In My Room

In My Room

Designing

For and

With Children

▼

ANTONIO F. TORRICE, ASID;

AND

RO LOGRIPPO

FAWCETT COLUMBINE ● NEW YORK

A Fawcett Columbine Book
Published by Ballantine Books

Photo and illustration credits can be found at the back of this book.

Library of Congress Cataloging-in-Publication Data

Torrice, Antonio F., 1951–
  In my room.

  Bibliography: p.
  Includes index.
  1. Children's rooms.   2. Interior design.
I. Logrippo, Ro, 1946–   . II. Title.
NK2117.C4T6   1989   747.7′7   88–47818
ISBN 0–449–90193–9

Interior Design by Michaelis/Carpelis Design Assoc. Inc.

Manufactured in Japan

First Edition: October 1989

10   9   8   7   6   5   4   3   2

TONY'S DEDICATION

*To Nana Frankini, who taught me so
clearly that you are never too old to
have a happy childhood.
To my parents, Joe and Yolanda,
who taught me through their example
the magic of endless love.
And to Michael, who taught me the joy
of sharing your very best.*

▼▼▼▼▼▼

RO'S DEDICATION

*To my parents, Rose and Jim, who
filled my earliest rooms with so much
love and laughter . . .
To my husband, Mike, who always
fills my heart with the spirit that culti-
vates inner growth . . .
And to my dearest friends, especially Tony, who never fail to fuel my
imagination with the burning desire to
dream and then to do.*

▼▼▼▼▼▼

Contents

Acknowledgments

▼▼▼▼▼▼

Some extraordinary people deserve special thanks for their contributions to this book.

Our gratitude goes to Carol Mann for recognizing early on the merits of publishing this work, and to Michelle Russell and Karen Hwa, our editors at Ballantine, for their warm support, enthusiasm and professional guidance.

Appreciation for carefully reading and critiquing the manuscript, all or in part, is extended to Michael Staron, Mike Spinelli, Stephen Pouliot, Teddi Grant Huseini and Terry Davenport Nagel. To Linda Runion, ASID, we extend special thanks for lending a professional ear and encouraging words long distance.

Our thanks for the part they played in the publishing process goes to Joelle Delbourgo, Nancy Hogan, Polin Cohanne, Joel Golub and Joyce Jansen.

We warmly acknowledge the support of Joseph, Yolanda, Margaret and J. R. Torrice, and Sam and Sue Spinelli, along with Robert Garlington and Kevin Yarbrough.

Thanks also to the parents of all the children that have contributed through the years to the success of Just Between Friends, and to the following professional organizations for the encouragement they have lent: the American Society of Interior Designers, the Institute of Business Designers, the International Furnishings and Design Association and the San Francisco Decorator Showcase.

For being motivational forces along the way, much gratitude is extended to Linda H. Harris, Carolyn Mady, Charles McCarthy, Mary Ellen de Andrea, Edward Pepan, Helen Fuson, Becky Pirelli and Stephanie Beard Gale.

In My Room

Introduction

▼▼▼▼▼

Looking back, I realize that children have taught me the greatest lessons in life.

From them, I've rediscovered the wonderment of youthful spontaneity, innocence and the kind of positive energy that makes you believe you can do anything.

My own childhood, spent in the rural New England house built by my grandfather, an Old World building contractor, nurtured a belief that nooks and crannies were safe refuges in a grown-up world. Blessed with a "secret hideaway" (the closet cubicles in the room I shared with my brother), I often enveloped myself in a textured cocoon of winter coats and Sunday finery. What further fed my imagination were assorted stone statuaries in our rock garden. All fabricated from custom molds my mother's father originally made for his construction projects, these miniature monuments transported me to a make-believe milieu where anything I fathomed was possible.

Beyond my own childhood, I immersed myself in a youth-centered environment as a college student majoring in early education, human development and theater arts. For four years at Villanova University, groups of emotionally disturbed, severely retarded and physically disabled children, as well as nonhandicapped children, shared their unique perspectives of the world with me.

During my sophomore through senior years, I lived with fifty-seven emotionally troubled five- to twelve-year-olds at the Devereux Foundation in Devon, Pennsylvania. As I endeavored to get these children to express themselves as part of their therapy, I realized that understanding a child's perspective required viewing it from his or her physical vantage point. While I strove as a preprofessional intern to keep peace in this suburban Philadelphia residential treatment center, I observed the difficulty that my charges had in feeling at home in the rooms they shared, devoid of any personal preferences, including color. Their impersonal quarters had insufficient space for storing games or toys or other individual possessions. Furthermore, these children told me, the places they occupied had another major flaw. Clocks and pictures were hung at adult viewing range—too high for young eyes to see without straining.

Watching these troubled children grow, I learned that their environment always mattered to them. Wanting their belongings secure and close at hand wasn't all that counted. So did privacy. Even in shared quarters, that meant having some secluded area to play and study and read.

The time I spent away from Devereux was devoted to preschoolers through the Montessori program at Ravenhill Academy in Germantown, Pennsylvania. While studying learning methods to become a Montessori teacher, I became fascinated with the need that young ones have for order in their lives. For example, if it was easy for children to find their belongings, they enjoyed keeping them stored in an orderly fashion when not in use. By their actions, these two- to five-year-old Montessori learners drove home a compelling message: Children are more apt to keep their work and play areas neat when those areas are accessible to them. When they are inaccessible, children vent their frustrations, leaving their belongings in disarray.

I became even more enlightened about other aspects of child behavior while working with severely retarded and physically disabled children. Instructing both groups on weekends at a Pennsylvania state hospital, I learned that these wards of the state were just as uncomfortable with the cold institutional settings they called home as were outsiders who visited them. Thrust into austere, colorless environments, they felt depersonalized. From them, I discovered how much we respond to color and warm surroundings.

Through interactive play, my state hospital experiences taught me that hyperactive, nervous children reach out for calming colors like blues and greens. Passive children are more likely to gravitate toward reds and oranges for a tonic effect. It was my specialized work with these young ones that earned me Villanova's Thomas J. Mentzer Memorial Award in 1973 and motivated me later in life to study the effects of color and light on humans.

My education in the ways of children took an interesting turn when I relocated to the West Coast after earning a bachelor's degree in child development and early education. Pursuing artistic interests because educational work was scarce at the time, I accepted a position at Design Research in San Francisco. This innovative home furnishings firm paved the way in the United States for the European concept of design best described as "form follows function." In other words, for a material object to be considered well made, it not only must be aesthetically pleasing, but practical. What that meant at D/R was imported "no frills" merchandise: modular furniture, stackable dinnerware and educational toys—mainstays that kept the company popular in nine locations coast to coast.

The handful of years I spent at D/R were devoted to visual merchandising and display, some of it directly related to children's items. My work kept me ever aware of the way color attracts people, regardless of age. And it kept me especially vigilant about rearranging merchandise to entice onlookers to interact with playthings and gadgetry.

Armed with knowledge about child development, I delighted in creating window displays that lured little ones and their par-

ents into D/R to play with imported puzzles and toys—gadgets that challenged the dexterity of growing hands. By the time I left the firm to pursue display work with varied business clients on an independent basis, I had become the company's national co-director of visual merchandising. I also had gained experience in the methods of inspiring young and old to try something new.

The opportunity to mesh my mixed backgrounds of child development and interior design presented itself in 1979 when a linen showroom client and I teamed up on a major Bay Area project. Together, we created a three-room setting for a six-year-old as part of a San Francisco benefit house tour that proved how a derelict mansion could be renovated by a team of talented professionals.

Joining forces on the metamorphosis we engineered was the client's daughter, Allison, a first grader, eager to share her ideas on the perfect quarters for someone her age. Brainstorming with us on almost every aspect of decor—from sleeping surface to window shades—this pint-size innovator opened our eyes to the wisdom of consulting with the young on the rooms they occupy.

"Suite Allison," a dream world where giant bunnies roamed and hand-painted carrot patches sprouted, not only fulfilled the environmental fantasies of the little girl in whose honor the rooms were named, but it also reflected the knowledge I gained from all the special children I had ever encountered. Above all, it proved how an

adult and child could interact to create a room devised from make-believe and based on real needs.

That San Francisco Decorator Showcase setting marked a turning point in my career. It gave birth to a business I call Just Between Friends, dedicated to creating "living and learning environments" with children's input every step of the way. From the onset, it broke with the conventional design method sanctioning adults to impose their tastes on children's decor. In so doing, it challenged the popular practice of turning havens for the young into magical domains like space stations or sport kingdoms or other theme lands that tend to time-lock a room. Instead, Just Between Friends championed the cause of children controlling their living quarters by permitting them to pick the palette that would permeate their world, then determine its layout. Since initiating my unique approach to children's design, I've had the opportunity to co-design with young ones from infancy up. I've had the chance to join forces with children of myriad abilities or challenges.

Receiving the 1985 Human Environment Award from the American Society of Interior Designers and top honors in the 1987 Halo Lighting Competition has given my concepts national exposure. Since then, I've had the exceptional experience of working not only with hospitals around the United States reshaping pediatric wards, but also with day-care centers and school facilities consulting on design issues. Through nationwide design seminars and programs, and major magazine articles, I've had the good fortune to share my theories and successful experiences on a subject that continues to enthrall and inspire me.

Putting children in charge of their own spaces is what this book is all about. Since they spend more time in their own rooms than anyone else, they should be the primary judges of how these rooms look and how they suit their needs. If children invest time creating their environment, I know from experience they'll invest time there and energy in its upkeep. Moreover, they'll experience the wonderment of active participation in a world that too often relegates them to a passive role, particularly in front of the television.

You might be asking, "Don't good parents know the best way to decorate a room for their children?" Regardless of how conscientious or how design-conscious parents may be, children need to identify at least part of the world around them as a space that they've devised right down to the color of the walls and the function of

furnishings. In the room they call "mine," they need to explore who they are, what they are and where they are. That's why in their rooms, whether shared or not, they need to be able to recreate their fantasies, not Mom's or Dad's.

Although children perform the lead roles in this scenario, their parents act more like cast members than rapt audience. In their supporting roles, they ask questions, draw diagrams, provide paint and carpet swatches and carry out the master plans the main characters concoct.

An undertaking such as this demands time and energy. But it need not demand your life savings. It's possible to work within a modest budget that can afford only paint and minor acquisitions. A larger investment, however, may enable you to create a room that "grows" with your child, with furnishings that convert to accommodate growing bodies and changing tastes.

By letting children control the environment where they spend the most time, you establish their self-confidence and securi-

ty. Only when young ones see that they can have an effect on their surroundings will they cultivate the positive feelings essential to mastering the world around them.

As you read these pages, you'll learn step by step how to collaborate with five- to twelve-year-olds to turn their young dreams into reality. You will learn first by opening your adult mind to their childlike ideas, and, finally, by translating their notions into workable plans. In the process of building their dream world, you will also build their self-esteem. Beyond that, you will strengthen your special bond with each other.

By listening to your children, you'll unravel all the information that will serve as the building blocks of your children's future.

I've learned much about the world through children. Through this book, so can you.

—Antonio F. Torrice,
ASID

PART ONE

Just Between Friends

Children as Co-Designers of Personal Space

▼▼▼▼▼

Suite Allison

"I liked the loft because it was like another bed. It was higher and I liked being high up because I could look at everything. It was like your own little room by yourself."
—Allison at fourteen

"Everyone remembered 'Suite Allison,' wishing they had a room like that—a fantasy room."
—Allison's father, Carl

For six-year-old Allison, interior design was a game of make-believe.

When I asked her to close her eyes and share her picture of a perfect room . . . presto! She imagined a brigade of bunnies guarding an inner sanctum. Just like a magician pulling cottontails from a hat, out of nowhere she seemed to yank giant Peter Rabbit look-alikes that hopped into position around the room.

When I coaxed her to tell me more about the scene . . . bingo! She saw a patch of Flopsy's favorite food sprouting on the walls. As she talked, a medley of hand-painted carrots appeared to dance near the ceiling.

Just fairy tales and fantasies for a child intent on battling things that go bump in the night?

Not for this little one. And not for 14,000 other people who saw "Suite Allison" on a San Francisco house tour over a decade ago.

But dancing carrots and prancing rabbits were only part of that corner bedroom at the 1979 San Francisco Decorator Showcase. What visitors to that area of the annual event also saw were a myriad of colorful activity centers for drawing and dancing, studying and staging tea parties, prettying up and pretending. All of them reflected a little girl's custom touches.

Yet more than young Allison's vivid imagination turned her dreams into reality. What did the trick were two grown-ups who had the sense to let a first grader show them how a child's imagination could unleash itself in a child's room.

Allison's father, Carl, a linen entrepreneur spotlighting his finest showroom lines in the fundraiser, and I, the business friend behind his store's visual displays, convinced the house tour's sponsors to allow us to transform a corner suite in the ramshackle mansion into a young girl's refuge. Like thirty-two other members of the design community pooling their talents for the three week undertaking, I would be expected to give that area a major face-lift.

The purpose: to entice the public to see the metamorphosis while raising money for charity in the process.

Young Allison's illusions never included nationwide attention. But by the time her seventh birthday rolled around, she had joined the ranks of professionally published interior designers. That happened when the home furnishings editors of *House Beautiful*, *Better Homes and Gardens* and *Designers West* previewed the site. Fortunately for me, they took more than a cursory glance at a six-year-old's dream come true. Within months, the pages of the magazines they represented featured our work prominently, proving the wisdom of letting a child decorate his or her domain. By then, Allison had another feather in her cap: the launching of my new business. Just Between Friends emerged as a design venture dedicated to "living and learning environments" masterminded by the small fry who would inhabit them.

And my role?

Call me the translator, the implementer. I would convert children's ideas into real spaces. Beyond that, I would be the grown-up who would listen intently to their fantastic notions and make them materialize right before their eyes—just like I did with Allison in the suite named in her hon-

or. And just like any parent can do who's willing to collaborate with a child on his or her personal living quarters.

Tapping Allison's tastes was never meant to be more than a one-time experiment. Carl and I had our own ideas about decorating a little girl's room with an adjacent bath and dressing area. We were primarily interested in promoting his business since the specialty shop had been exclusive to the design trade until then.

Before Allison entered the picture, Carl and I envisioned the rooms we would fabricate resplendent in imported French fabric. The imaginary princess who would reign there would dwell in a tidy chamber steeped in frills for sleep and stocked in regal supplies for study and storage.

In theory, it sounded enchanting. But after submitting a rough sketch of the room for our mythical miss, we realized the folly of two grown men conjecturing about the wishes of a nonexistent little girl. A real child conceivably could make the room, well, more realistic.

And Allison fit the bill.

As her father reasoned, "Allison was a way to humanize our design."

Although only six, this young family friend was quite articulate, expressing herself with much animation. Quickly, our friendship grew. But then, what child wouldn't strike up a better acquaintance with someone helping her concoct the bedroom of her dreams?

We only meant to ask Allison for a few suggestions, but she was smart and seized the opportunity for expression. Almost ev-

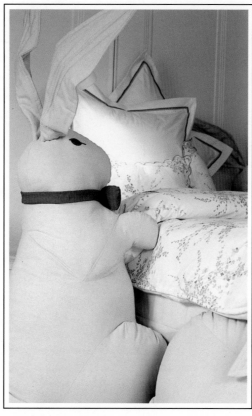

Stuffed play pals offer a sense of security and companionship.

erything about the empty space we showed her evoked opinions as she investigated existing cubbyholes.

"If this were your room," I quizzed her, "what would you want in it?"

It was a loaded question, eliciting plenty of responses. For example:

• Rabbits should protect the sleeping area. Not just any garden variety hippety-hoppers. Only "washable" rabbits were acceptable! "I just love rabbits," Allison declared. (We settled for soft sculpture canvas ones, or, as Allison called them, "big stuffed animals." Almost her size, they also could serve as furniture for her and her small friends.)

• The bed itself should be "marshmallow soft" and steeped in comfy coverings doubling as someplace to hide. Besides that, she told us, it should look "real pretty."

• And the colors? Adults probably would have opted for the delicate palette then popular. But the primary student preferred primary colors—namely, marmalade and mint. In fact, green and orange already had been decided upon as a scheme and accepted by the showcase committee when Allison came upon the scene. But she got to pick the intensity of those colors that would predominate.

The walls were dressed in Allison's green. Her orange surfaced atop two large windows where a row of carrots were painted as an ornamental border described as a "dado." Since a bunch of ten tap-danced over both panes, we christened her quarters a twenty-carrot bedroom! "I thought they were real neat," Allison later mused about her bunny brigade's food.

Nor did Allison's input end when the space was dutifully appointed. She was exasperated at discovering that the Roman shades were attached in standard fashion to the top of the windows so they could fold up and down like an accordion with a pull cord. Mustering her six-year-old savvy, she challenged my logic, wanting to

A 6-year-old provided the inspiration for "Suite Allison," a showcase setting that proved that children and adults can join to create imaginative environments reflecting real needs.

know why they couldn't be hung from the bottom up! And why not? It was the only way someone her size could manage to use them.

Furthermore, the little girl sighed, she couldn't reach the books placed high on the shelving. Nor could she find anyplace to keep her jewelry.

Talk about constructive criticism!

The more I listened to this grade school marvel, the more I remembered my college days spent studying childhood behavior and working with emotionally disturbed five- to twelve-year-olds. I was reminded of that important lesson about the young: When you try to view life from their vantage point, view it from their physical level. Don't put a clock too high on the wall. Or anything else for that matter.

Lower yourself to child height and you can tell what's out of reach or out of sight. Carl understood the merits of using this method with Allison. "For her, it was like having a talented playmate suddenly listening to all you say and translating it."

Watching Allison organize her world reminded me of a Montessori lesson. Simply put, order is important in children's lives. Allow them to create order in a room through accessible storage, and establish an easy, enjoyable way for keeping things in place.

ACTIVITY CENTERS

Conversations with Allison sparked the orderly activity centers in "Suite Allison."

Whether they're weather instruments or toy dinosaurs, childhood acquisitions serve as learning tools in an activity center for a nature-loving boy or girl.

By paying attention, I learned her preferences for the world around her.

Prisms. Plants. Puzzles. Musical instruments. Maps. All that and more mesmerized this little girl and prompted me to devote space to each specific area of interest.

There were study areas to absorb science and math . . . an art area to explore creativity and show off youthful artwork . . . a ballet bar to practice pliés . . . a Mother Nature space to investigate living things . . . a tea party place to amuse playmates or doll friends . . . a dress-up section to study her appearance in a wall mirror . . . a gallery for viewing photo blowups that captured a budding dancer's life.

Each of these centers could be considered tools for new discoveries and adventures in a constantly unfolding world.

Not all of Allison's amassed treasures were hers, I confess. Some were my very own designs, custom-made by craftsmen after sharing childhood memories of toys that amused me. Most were wooden jigsaw puzzles that challenged the dexterity of growing hands and encouraged growing minds to learn proportion.

Like the special Massachusetts home where I grew up with its secret spaces, Allison's suite had a very special alcove. It was a combination sleeping/playing/hiding loft above the shelves in the dressing room where her wardrobe was tucked into one corner and her art supplies and easel into another, naturally at a safe distance from the clothes.

Circus stripes on a shower curtain make as much of a personal statement as monogrammed towels.

To reach the loft, the child climbed a ladder and entered a world where some days make-believe friends presumably visited. At other times, a private hideaway existed.

"It was like your own little room by yourself," Allison confides today. "I liked being up high because I could look at everyone. It was kind of cozy being by myself."

To keep the art area clutter-free, white laminate wire shelving hung low so that a child could easily pluck precious things. But art supplies weren't the only items within Allison's grasp. As she remarks, "I didn't have to reach for anything. That whole room was my height. It was great!"

The rest of Allison's three-room suite likewise reflected her personality. Little girl's frilly fashions filled the dressing area which was differentiated from the main room by paint color. Its walls were carrot orange and its woodwork trim, like the rest of the setting, was crisp white.

In the bathroom, the walls were awash with blue. But bright touches abounded from rainbow colors in the soaps and bath salts to circus stripes in shower curtains and towels, monogrammed by her dad's shop with Allison's name, of course.

If ever I hesitated before the showcase opened to let a little girl dictate how to decorate a little girl's space, I had only to watch Allison show off the space to her mother, Barbara, who privately boasted of her daughter's experience. "It was a great addition to her life. She was being asked what her values were, what her ideas were. And it made her feel very important, giving her a lot of pride and self-worth."

A CHILD'S INPUT

Barbara's words and Allison's actions fired my faith in the importance of a child's input in his or her environment. As I witnessed the six-year-old rearranging things to suit her fancy, I realized how much she'd changed since the room's transformation began. This bright little one knew from the start this habitat truly wasn't her own. Yet, watching her paper plans become reality, she soon acclimated to and mastered her surroundings.

It was all the proof I needed to develop this premise: the more you allow a young one to invest time and energy in his or her personal environment, the more that child will want to invest time being there, playing there and learning there. From that point on, a child will have a stake in the maintenance of that room, just as Allison illustrated when she lingered to reorganize the decor at each visit.

As part of her play during these sessions, she would study her image in three life-size photographs on the wall. As she stared at herself poised in ballet positions, her smile seemed to say, "I love these."

Allison actually never would spend a night in the namesake setting that reflected her signature. But she would get another chance to design her own room when her family moved, not long after "Suite Allison" had become just a memory.

THE THREE C's

By the time Allison and I collaborated on her actual bedroom, I had begun developing a formula for extracting children's ideas of their dream spaces and for translating them into reality. There were three essential ingredients to making those spaces work: *choice*, *color* and *convertibility*.

Often overlooked, these three C's tend to be the most important principles in designing a child's space.

- By *choice*, I mean the process of allowing a child to define his desires for a dream world he will inhabit.
- By *color*, I mean drawing out the special part of the rainbow in which the child wishes to surround himself.
- By *convertibility*, I mean designing with adaptability in mind so that a space can grow up, too, as the child stretches toward adulthood.

Choice. Color. Convertibility. These three keys unlock the doors of children's imaginations and open their minds to the real world awaiting the significant contributions they can make.

CHAPTER 2

Mapping Choices

Like a seedling waiting for the sun so it could grow, young Michael lingered between two worlds.

A wide-eyed child grasping verbal sounds, the three-and-a-half-year-old was intensely curious yet bashful. Silently, he would watch someone visiting the house interact with his parents; then cautiously, he would establish eye contact. It was obvious the timid boy not so secretly longed to be part of the dialogue. If only he could express himself....

Little could Michael have imagined that his mastery of language was just a simple coloring sketch away.

Little could his parents have dreamed that the drawing's recreation as his environment would help transform their shy son into an outgoing, talkative child.

Transporting Michael to the world of words was a journey that began and ended in the room he called "mine." En route, the scenery changed from a jumbled juvenile circus to a private place steeped in an adventurous boy's personal interests in puppetry, painting and playing with puzzles. Upon reaching his final destination, Michael not only improved his communication skills, but also felt more self-confident and secure—a direct result of having seen his childish scribbles take shape as his room.

"I like this shelf because I can climb it. It's very useful."

—*Michael at eight*

"Michael was a shy child. He understood a great deal, but he wasn't able to communicate it effectively. And the room just opened him up."

—*Michael's mother, Marshia*

Watching this little one unfold while his surroundings changed considerably was my professional privilege. I entered Michael's quiet world because of caring parents who wanted to assure him of his important place in the family circle. At first, my young client and I communicated nonverbally from the same vantage point—his bedroom floor. Munching home-baked cookies, we formed the pleasant bond that comes from sharing food and other experiences.

GAMEPLAYING

Eager to interact with my new friend, I played a game based on ordinary doodles.

With a sketch pad and colored markers in hand, I closed my eyes and made a random scribble on the paper, embellishing it slightly when I peeked at what I'd done. Purposely, before anything recognizable took form, I handed the pad over to my playmate so he could continue the picture in any fashion with any colored marker he preferred. Back and forth. Back and forth. The game continued with each of us enjoying the other's rudimentary artistry. If a bird or a car or any other object would start to materialize, I'd add a new dimension to alter the drawing, thereby encouraging the child to fantasize and foster new ideas.

Interacting in such a way with Michael, I discovered what a whiz he was on paper. I also confirmed my art therapy training, which taught how powerful this kind of visualization is with children.

Besides gaining the boy's acceptance of me as a friend, this playful activity lowered his guard. Soon there were giggles and laughs that let me know a spirited soul existed beneath that reserve.

As the game continued, I employed another tactic to let Michael know we were on the same wavelength. Looking at one, then another of my scribbles, he would whisper: "Sure looks like a silly duck to me." And I'd respond in like manner: "Yes,

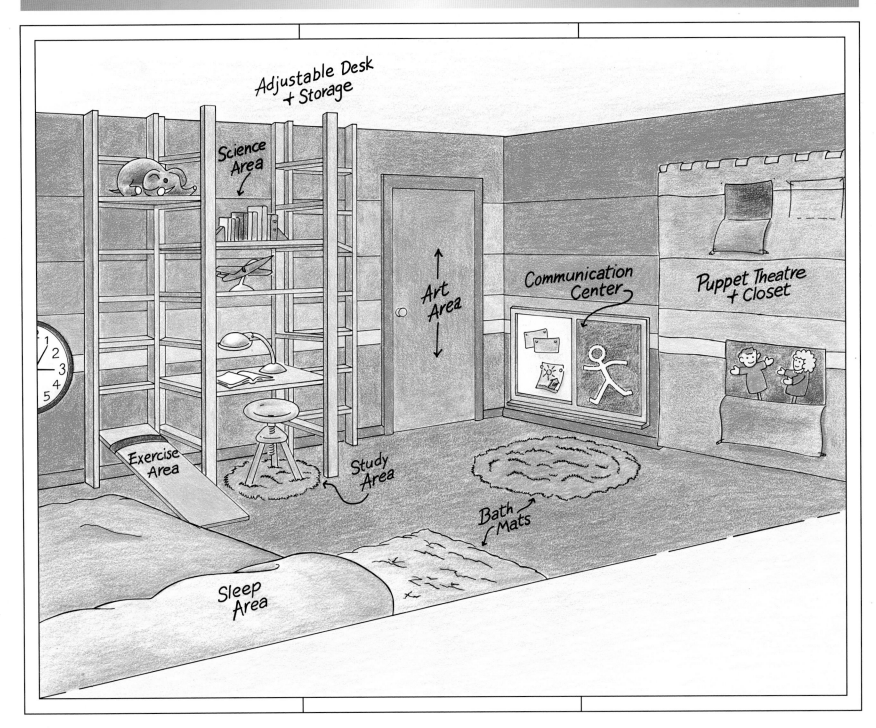

what a silly duck he is." By using similar language, I let him know that I understood his vocabulary.

Comfortable with each other now, we had established a rapport that would allow for serious interaction. "Tell me," I asked him straightforwardly, "where do you sleep?" Not a word was uttered, but in response, as if I'd directed him to show me, he walked past a single bed and stood near the crib he would soon outgrow. Gently, I continued the questioning, asking such things as, "Where are you going to sleep when you leave that crib?" and "Where do your clothes go?" Each time I questioned him about his world, he began play acting by physically going over to the space in question. Sometimes he just pointed, but always he got into the theater of the moment by smiling and performing in pantomime fashion. Fascinated, I kept up the dialogue, this time prodding him to tell me where new things should be placed, like a desk or a clock or a container for dirty clothes.

As I watched Michael position himself around the room, I studied his actions, intent on discovering his limitations as well as his abilities in this eleven-by-thirteen-foot space. I looked to see how easily he could maneuver himself from one side of the room to the other. And I paid close attention to how readily accessible his belongings were, making notes on the simple room sketch I was drawing in black crayon.

By doing these exercises with Michael, I realized that being quiet hadn't hindered his comprehension of his surroundings.

With that in mind, I took the next step in reshaping his world with his input. Fanning before him six cards deeply saturated in different shades of the color spectrum, I asked him if he would play one final game with me. "If you could have one of these cards," I asked, "which one would you pick?" Spontaneously, he reached for the color green.

Ready to expand my knowledge of Michael by being with him outdoors, I encouraged play between us. Like a bird in flight, he seemed to spread wings in the midst of nature, making giddy noises and yelling excitedly. Quickly, I learned how coordinated he was as he proudly showed off what his body could do by tossing and catching balls, jumping up and down and running free.

The mastery Michael exhibited in his outdoor living playground convinced me that his indoor learning playground should incorporate the opportunity for physical fitness. A firm believer in the oneness of mind and body, I know the importance of combining both aspects in human environment. One cannot exist without the other, especially in a child's world where encouraging both can promote a lifetime of fitness.

Remarkably, by the time Michael and I ended our outdoor play, he'd begun to open up and verbally communicate with me. Indeed, the bashful boy I'd met just an hour earlier had given way to a conversive child. Small wonder by the time I was almost ready to depart, I had a new friend anxious for my return.

PARENTAL INPUT

Because a child's room is connected to the rest of the house, as the child is connected to the rest of the family, I touched base with Michael's parents before leaving to receive input on budget and other considerations that they felt were essential. Extras they wanted in their son's room included laundry, cleanup and music areas (the latter to nurture sound appreciation), as well as additional storage and lighting (especially by the bed to encourage reading).

Armed with all this information, I devised plans between visits for incor-

Safe, efficient coat hooks help keep this cleanup area free of clutter.

porating many changes in Michael's room. Giving equal value to what child and parent wanted, I assembled ideas and a shopping list to implement them.

SPECIAL SPACES

Enthusiastically welcomed on my second trip to Michael's home, I had no difficulty engaging him in conversation. Spreading out a basic black-and-white sketch that looked like the kind from coloring books, I showed the thoughtful youngster the preliminary plans for his room with furnishings arranged, as suggested, just where he wanted them. And following parental directives, special spaces were devoted to clean-up tools and other needs.

What Michael also saw in his preliminary plan was a spot where the collection of puppets he treasured could come alive. Realizing how puppetry as a performance art encourages speech skills, I had provided a site where small hands could animate cloth characters. This puppet theater was simply a sturdy canvas cloth slit with three openings. It hung in place of the closet door, moving back and forth on a round curtain rod. Behind the canvas stage, there was room for traditional clothing storage as well as a hideaway loft with safety bars and cushions that invited young nappers. Located where the standard top shelf would be, the loft would be accessible to a growing tyke from the dowels of a built-in ladder system on one side.

Reconfigured to accommodate an active, growing frame, this closet does more than store clothes within easy child reach. It acts as an exercise area for climbers intent on retreating to a reading loft. Sturdy dowels perform double duty as ladder rungs and safety bars in this built-in system.

A standard closet becomes a special space when the door is replaced with a canvas cloth slit to create a puppet stage. Besides fostering performance skills and fantasy play, the makeshift stage encourages speech and communication. Hung on a simple curtain rod, the fabric glides back and forth so belongings kept inside are still accessible.

LEARNING CENTERS

Having learned from "Suite Allison" how vital personalized learning centers are to the success of a child's room, I designed several for Michael, tailor-made to his interests. Besides the puppet theater, there were four other mini environments for art, exercise, sensory play and science.

The Art Learning Center is where crayons, scissors, paints and Popsicle sticks would intermingle. A versatile area for expression, it would include a giant clipboard and drawing paper to hang on the back of the door. Adjacent to it would be a young master's message center with wall-hung chalkboard and corkboard for posting artwork and messages from Mom.

The Exercise Center would contain a thick foam-covered slant board for stretching growing muscles and climbing, while the Sensory Play Center would be the focal point for sound, smell, taste, touch and sight.

Measuring, magnifying and weighing gear share space in this science center.

Michael's fifth area—the Science Learning Center—would allow his inquisitive mind to study shapes, sizes and nature objects that mesmerized him. Rocks, leaves and shells would find a home here alongside scientific gadgetry such as prisms, pocket microscopes and weather instruments.

While his young mind absorbed all this information, I quizzed Michael again on his preferences for the location of everything, wanting to be sure that he was comfortable with the planned arrangement. If he didn't like something where it was, such as the wall clock, we discussed alternatives. In this way, we developed our makeshift blueprint.

Explaining that Mom and Dad would have the final say, I made no unkeepable promises to the child. But I left him on a playful note, once again asking that he pick a colored card from the rainbow assortment I fanned before him. This time, Michael chose orange, telling me later he was aware

Hanging sketch pad and chalkboard localize artistic play. Other tools include a corkboard large enough to handle art work, photos and/or family messages.

Choice, color and convertibility blend in this setting where a young boy's "signatures" range from life-size paper cutouts to a custom-painted arch.

that green was his choice the day we first met. Clearly, this was an indication that Michael hadn't changed his mind. Rather, he wanted his personal environment to be more than just *one* color.

This time before leaving, I gave Michael and his parents their own copies of the preliminary sketch to enable them to make changes before the design was finalized. As it turned out, his parents made several minor alterations. At their suggestion, what could have been built-in storage along the base of their child's new bed was redesigned as a sleeping trundle to accommodate an overnight guest. Because sunlight was inadequate, the large indoor plant originally envisioned next to the sleeping area was reconsidered. In its place were put a stack of colorful plastic milk carton carriers that could do double duty as storage for building blocks.

Decorations might include whimsical mobiles like this smiling paper sun.

Some things in Michael's room were purely whimsical. So that he could awaken to a smiling face, a large paper sun with a golden grin was hung over the bed. For special company, he could look even closer at three life-size paper cutouts of his human form in his special colors. The boyish images he and his mother fashioned from craft paper were coated with poster paints and hung on the wall over the bed where they appeared to grasp the reading lights.

Caught up in the excitement of creating brand new quarters, Michael seemed to love everything. When I departed, his wide eyes danced with anticipation.

While the puppeteer dreamed of the shows he might stage in his future domain, I searched for furnishings that would make his dream room happen. But the marketplace didn't satisfy my objectives. It seemed that children's furnishings were either painted or covered with decals following juvenile themes that inevitably time-lock a room. What wasn't decorated in cartoon characters was either too traditional to suit young tastes or custom-made and too expensive. Instead of opting for any of these, I found skilled craftsmen to execute my own designs—modular systems styled with stackability and convertibility in mind so that they literally could grow with a child.

Part of what that meant in Michael's room was a combination desk and shelf unit with adjustable ladderlike components. As Michael's physical frame reached new heights, so, too, could his work station. And as he yearned for treasures stored

Adjustable ladderlike components allow work stations to grow with the child.

up high, he could climb rung by rung and reach for them.

SIGNATURES

Furnishings were just part of what would bring the picture of Michael's future world into focus. My mission was also to obtain a range of paint chips so that he could pick the palette that would color his kingdom. In Michael's case, that translated to samples of orange and green so he could zero in on the shades he liked best.

At the final session, I would present my

young client with his working plans, pointing to the paint chips and instructing him to select where his colors lay along the spectrum. Like a thermometer registering the temperature, the chips Michael would choose would tell me how hot or how cold the colors of orange and green would be in his room. It made no difference if his selections matched the original cards he chose in our first two sessions. What mattered was the opportunity for him to redefine the color by looking at a range from light to dark.

Describing Michael's dream room in fairy-tale fashion was a pint-size production at the kitchen table when my show-and-tell day finally arrived. Spinning my storyline from a brightly colored green-and-orange portfolio, I opened up this book of images, unveiling all the props, from paint chips to carpet swatches to furniture brochures. As the tale of Michael's future room unfolded, my audience burst into applause. Clearly, they were ready to stage this production.

In Michael's case, I had expounded upon this child's gifts and then took them a step further. This "once upon a time" tale really would find the main character living "happily ever after." Eager to seal a magic moment, I handed the young star effecting these changes his well-deserved reward—a box of eight brightly colored crayons. Now, he really could determine how chromatic his world would be.

As I explained to those assembled, since Michael had chosen orange and green, he should use only those two crayons first in

Toy bins facilitate upkeep in the bedroom. Small playthings are well-suited to such storage.

filling in the room's sketch I provided. When his parents felt he had used orange and green everywhere he wanted, then they were to replace them with the rest of the crayons so the boy could continue coloring. The finished work would be delivered to me so I could set the plan in motion.

Like someone unveiling a major artwork, I marveled a short time later when I saw what Michael had applied to his paper canvas. Impressed by his ability to capture

details and transpose them into form, I stared in amazement when I saw what the three-and-a-half-year-old had done to the walls. To visually lower the ceiling so it wouldn't tower as much over the child, I had detailed the walls on all sides with wide stripes. Like the carrot border in "Suite Allison," the bands would achieve a "dado effect" when painted a contrasting color from the rest of the wall. But instead of coloring just one band or several in assorted colors, Michael had taken the time to systematically shade them all in gradations of orange, resembling the paint chips in his portfolio. His personal imprint also was apparent in the floor area where he had completely colored with a green crayon around several mats that were in the sketch. Of course, I thought to myself, a child spending as much time as he does playing on the floor would enjoy exploring on grassy green carpeting. I truly had met a budding designer!

The way Michael or any child chooses to color their personal place is particularly significant and just as unique as the way they sign their names. For that reason, I call this phase of the choice process *signatures*. More than any other aspect of children's room design, the use of *signatures* will drive home the message that young ones can change and adapt their environment.

Michael's colorful sketch contained one other element that made an important statement. In the closet and the exercise area, purple had been scribbled intensely. From art therapists, I had learned that the

Labeling objects with peel-off vinyl letters makes learning language an easier and more enjoyable task.

use of the color purple may signify something unfamiliar to a child. In Michael's case, the slant board seemed rather foreboding until its function was explained to him. So, too, did the closet with its canvas door. Once he was reassured that there was nothing to worry about and shown how the puppet stage operated, his troubles evaporated.

FINISHING TOUCHES

Anxious to see his make-believe story come true, Michael was ever vigilant while workers carried out his designs. Caught up in the activity of frenzied construction, he had a hand in the implementation of his color choices on the walls. As painters pre-pared to rim the room in bands of orange, the boy became fascinated as an arch resembling part of the rainbow was applied over his bed.

Nor was Michael the only one making refinements in the final stages. Watching everything take shape, I, too, fancied a finishing touch—large white vinyl peel-off labels to be placed on major objects so a boy learning language could practice vocabulary. They would spell out dozens of objects like desk, chair, broom and wastebasket. As these words were mastered, new ones could take their place around the room.

By the time Michael's room was completed, the boy behind it had truly blossomed. In a few short weeks, he had come to realize what a powerful influence choice can be. While his parents marveled at the lessons this experience had taught him, I also marveled at how much Michael had taught me about the impact a child's environment can have on human development.

Tucking the boy into bed on the first night in this setting, I toyed with his imagination, telling him what my grandma Nana Frankini once told me—make a wish on each corner of a new bed. Somehow, I knew one of those wishes already had come true.

A MASTER PLAN

Repeating Michael's success story in your own home is as easy as listening to what your children tell you about their private worlds. But it requires more than time and money to achieve the best results. It takes a *Master Plan* that spells out everything and reflects a child's input and a parent's approval.

Before approaching any child on such an important subject, evaluate the situation in that young one's room. Is it time to get rid of the crib and acquire other furnishings? Will the space be shared with a brother or sister? How much money can be spent for changes? All these questions need resolving before any dialogue with children begins.

Even if you can afford only minor details, you can provide a way for your children to make a meaningful impact on their special space. At the very least, a can of paint on a single wall will enable the little ones who choose its color to believe they have a stake in their surroundings. Intensify the feeling that much more by allowing them to go with you to the hardware store to pick paint chips and all the supplies. That exercise alone will set the mood for what's ahead.

Carpeting and bedcovers are other effective ways to alter children's rooms on limited budgets. By carpeting, I don't mean wall-to-wall necessarily; small area rugs like bath mats tossed over existing floor covering can create the same effect in a child's eyes as an overall look. So can small touches such as bright new desk blotters or bulletin boards wrapped in colorful fabric—two options well suited to renters.

But paint, carpeting and bed covers are the most effective inexpensive changes. If you can't buy all of them, invest in at least one to dramatize the effect. The bottom line to remember is the importance of letting children taste at least part of this experience, even if it's impractical for them to taste it all.

With all this in mind, find the best one-on-one time when your child is focused on listening to you and vice versa. It might be in the evening when the family gathers, or it might be just before a nap. Whatever is a good time for special discussion, make the most of it with the following exercise.

Gathering a brown or black marker pen plus a big brown shopping bag or a large clean piece of craft paper, situate yourself face-to-face on the floor in your child's room. Your vantage point is most impor-tant since you don't want to assume a superior physical position he or she might find intimidating.

While your child is watching, cut the bag open and draw a bird's-eye view of the room as if from the ceiling looking down. You don't have to draw it to scale, but you do have to draw it somewhat in proportion since it's crucial that components fit where indicated. Mark where windows and doors go as well as closets, outlets and air vents. A rudimentary floor plan, it should note the direction doors swing open. No crayons or colored pencils yet; they come later.

DOWN-TO-EARTH DIALOGUE

Once the overview is drawn, begin to ask the child specific things about the room. Talking in terms familiar to him or her, the conversation may sound like this:

"Where do you want to sleep in this room?"

"Where do you want to work?"

"Where do you put your toys?"

"Where do your clothes go?"

Don't be surprised if the answers to your questions are nonverbal expressions. Some children may prefer to point to different places in the room or on the sketch, while others may feel comfortable acting out responses in certain spots. In either situation, in the areas that were specified by the child, write the words "sleep," "work," "toy storage" and so forth.

After doing this map of the room, take a break. It's not important to get all of this done during your very first session. The project probably will be more successful if you give the child time to digest some of the decisions. Furthermore, parents should be alert to their child's attention span. Never try to do more than the child seems ready to handle. After all, you wouldn't simultaneously teach tying shoes, speaking French and adding numbers. It's counterproductive to do too much too soon. Better to accomplish one aspect at a time than to confuse the issue.

The next day (or whenever it seems appropriate), return to the same site for the second session. Now it's time to coax a little to discover more about those designated areas. "Well, what does that sleep area look like?" you might ask the child. "Is it high? Is it low? Is it a bunk bed or a canopy bed?" If it's a bunk, find out who sleeps where, discussing the problems that can occur on the top if a sleeper isn't careful. Safety is always an important issue and now may be the perfect time to cover related topics like fire, weather and earthquake precautions.

As you guide young ones through all the areas in their room, have them agree about the best location for items that likely will be kept there.

When looking at the work area, encourage the child to pinpoint where school supplies, arts and crafts projects or even pens and pencils should go. If they make these choices on their own and Mom and Dad adhere to them, it's very likely that, later, things will be kept just where both parent and child intended. Be sure to include reasons why some things might not work. For instance, if the child wants to fingerpaint next to the bed, explain what a problem that would be. "I think it really would be nice to have a place to paint," you might say, "but there's also a problem with that since paint stains the rugs and makes an awful mess. Let's put that somewhere it can't create those problems."

Don't be afraid to discuss something if the child makes an unrealistic request, like wanting a bed in front of the entry. Try to be patient, explaining why that just won't work. "If it's in front of the doorway, then you can't come in and play here because the bed will block your way," you might say. Or "If that's where the bed was and you were inside, you'd be stuck there and that would be terrible, because when it was time to go out and see your friends, you couldn't get out and they couldn't get in." Then, offer the child a reasonable alternative for consideration. By exchanging advice, you let the young one know there are some limits to this exercise.

As you go along, give the child a chance to interject ideas. Maybe he or she envisions something you wouldn't that could make this room extra special. Don't dismiss any young notion casually since all input should be deemed valuable. If it's preposterous, like a roller coaster, refrain from discrediting the idea or saying "no" outright. Instead, respond: "That won't work at this time, but let's put it in our future plan, and, as you grow older, take a look at it." Maybe by next year, the roller coaster will assume a different image. Or maybe

the carnival ride wasn't all that important to begin with but just a flight of fancy tossed out in an imaginative moment. What's paramount here is not so much a child's whimsy but his or her ease in expressing it.

From the beginning, understand that all suggestions and requests by a child are valid in that child's mind. And from the beginning a child should understand that sometimes affordability, availability and practicality prevent a parent from making things happen. In other words, freedom to choose a room to grow in doesn't mean license to put anything in it you want.

COLOR THE DREAM

Now that you and your child have created a more complete picture of what your child's room should look like, begin to resketch it, noting all the particulars. You don't need to possess Michelangelo's talents to do this. All that matters is getting the concepts you both have agreed upon down on paper simply and understandably. When that's done, you're ready to allow young ones to color their environment.

PICK A CARD

Using the six rainbow-colored cards contained at the back of this book, fan them out in the order they appear in the spectrum—red, orange, yellow, green, blue and

violet. Lay them flat on the table or on the floor side by side as you prepare to engage your child in the next activity.

"You can have one of these cards. Which one would you pick?" That's the first color question you pose, making sure not to prejudice a selection by suggesting there might be one correct answer. Don't rephrase the query by asking either "What color do you want me to paint your room?" or "What's your favorite color?" The whole idea revolves around their spontaneous selection of a card they really want the most. You don't want a child to think you're looking for the "right" answer. Nor do you want to imply that you hold an opinion about the selection.

That immediate response is the key to color magic so crucial to a child's surroundings. More than likely, you'll find it's easier to evoke that response the more relaxed a child is in the situation.

This color quiz should be repeated at every session in the same way. But don't be surprised if different cards are chosen at different times. Changing your mind isn't an option restricted to grown-ups, nor is wanting more than one color to appear in your personal place. Keep in mind, too, that other ideas are also subject to alteration. It's better to modify things now than when the furniture delivery truck arrives!

After playing this game once at each session, hand your child a copy of the black-and-white sketch and a box of eight crayons (red, orange, yellow, green, blue, violet, brown and black). Give instructions to fill in between the lines with only the crayon (or crayons) that match the colors picked in the game you played. Once you feel those colors have been used everywhere the budding artist wants, replace them with the rest of the crayons in the box. It's very important that the child's spontaneous color choices be used in the room first because what the child chooses first to decorate with those crayons will indicate the features of the room most important to that young mind. In Michael's room, they were the walls and the floor. In your child's room they could be anything. Whatever they are should serve as a cue, a *signature* if you will, of the child's innermost feelings about a space considered "mine." Later, when children see those coloring elements duplicated in their room, it will be apparent to them that they affected that design and therefore can affect their own lives.

If it seems natural to be part of the child's coloring experience as a silent witness, then do so. If not, leave the child alone to enjoy solitary play. A parent's important role here is showing interest so the child will feel comfortable with the task at hand.

Take a break now. The next step involves some homework at the hardware store. Hand in hand, lead your little one to the paint section, showing the assortment of paint chips available. Now, pick several chips closest in color to what your child favored in the color quiz. They don't necessarily need to match perfectly. What's important is giving the child a range from light to dark so the color preference can be redefined. Like someone listening to the ra-

dio, color selection is a two-phase process. First, you tune in to color waves like you would to sound waves when you tune the radio dial to the "right" station, be it jazz or rock or classical music. Next, you tune in to the right color intensity as you would turn the radio volume up or down to your preferred sound level.

Returning home, place all the paint chips together for the child's inspection. Just as I asked Michael, ask your little one to tell you how "loud" (dark) or how "quiet" (light) the color should be in the room.

If your child is inclined to pick more than one color paint chip, be open to the idea. Remember how Michael chose three shades of orange just for the walls? So, too, may the imaginative being who dwells with you.

Once the color chip preference has been established, it's time to return to the store to purchase the paint. But before you order exactly what your child picked, keep in mind that a tiny swatch of color will appear deeper and more intense on a large surface like a wall. For that reason, I suggest buying quart-size cans of several colors in close proximity in the spectrum. That way, a few can be tested on a wall before the child makes the final choice.

COMPROMISE

As a parent, you may consider the color your child chose as too powerful to suit your taste. In that case, you might want to limit its use to one wall, letting success or

the lack of it determine whether the rest of the room receives the same treatment. But, if you absolutely cannot tolerate the selection, be honest with the child. Simply say: "I have to live in this house, too, and I think I would feel very uncomfortable with that color." The child needs to recognize your relationship to the room. So, too, the child needs to realize a connection with the rest of the family. After all, this private domain was never meant to be an escape hatch.

Because you want children to articulate their own ideas, approach this interaction as a nurturing experience. That doesn't mean you have to invest in everything children say they want. Renovating their room is no excuse for overindulgence. While you want children to be free enough to go with all their fantasies, you want them to be realistic in their expectations. As a practical parent paying for this transformation, it's your task to weed out the essential elements, discarding the rest or modifying them to achieve the same results. Let's take a canopy bed as an example. Perhaps your little girl dreams of the day she can sleep in such elegant surroundings, but you know the expense is out of the question. You might be able to satisfy her, and your budget, by creating a small tented area somewhere in the room with a piece of fabric draped like a canopy from the ceiling.

A point to remember in all of this is that while you're expecting the child to paint a verbal picture of the perfect environment, that vision may not be necessarily the ideal. Perfect is their image of it. Ideal is the one that works for both of you.

That brings up another issue—the child who may not want a room changed at all. Just because Mom and Dad want to create a special space for their offspring is no reason for renovation to begin if there's no interest on the part of the child. It's entirely possible the surroundings are fine just the way they are in the child's eyes. But if problems exist like inadequate storage, tackle them by suggesting room reorganization rather than a complete makeover. Explain your reasoning and encourage the child to organize the setting to make space for toys or dirty clothes or whatever.

OLDER CHILDREN

As you might imagine, dealing with an older child on this subject is a different experience altogether. As they approach junior high, most elementary school students trade childhood fantasies for what they consider "grown-up" attitudes, relying on sources like television advertisers, magazines and friends. Although it seems they're programmed to respond to this stimulus, it's not impossible to tap their true feelings. It just takes time and patience to rekindle their personal imagination so real needs surface.

But time is on your side when you finally start working with older children on living arrangements. The "pick a card" process and all it entails may take only an hour or two since their mental capacity allows for translating a picture in their mind to a picture on paper in no time flat.

Because of their height, older children will require more storage space than younger ones to accommodate their longer clothes. Once taller, they also can reach shelves higher than they could when they

For musically inclined children, a center for records and instruments promotes this special interest.

were younger.

It's no secret that children in this age bracket are budding collectors, hoarding posters, cassette tapes and other paraphernalia. For that reason, they should localize their possessions just like younger children do in their personalized learning centers. Confining interests to a special area makes more sense than devoting the entire room to a central theme, since it's only natural a child of any age changes tastes periodically. Think about it. If the whole room is teddy bears or hot rods, they're always there, impossible to ignore.

INSTILLING
SELF-ESTEEM

No matter what the age, this interaction between you and your child should drive home the need for the person you brought into this world to decide on the looks of the private room he or she will inhabit. Too many parents create a room to fulfill their own childhood fantasies or to mimic a pretty picture they saw in a decorating magazine.

Allow children to change or adapt their environments and allow them to cultivate a sense of self-esteem. Instill that in them and watch how they master their world.

CHAPTER 3

Color My World

Curled up like a sleeping kitten, the young camper snuggled close to rustic floorboards, concentrating on the game at hand.

Encircling his small frame were twelve friendly faces, each awaiting his enactment of make-believe derring-do.

While the boy daydreamed of cars and castles, soft strains of music broke the stillness, and a solitary beam of violet light began shining overhead from makeshift stage lights.

Basking in his favored color, the playful child unraveled himself, acting out a tale of mighty dragons and mightier dragon slayers. Gazing at this fantasy production were two dozen eyes, including mine, intent on learning the innermost feelings of a boy besieged by a painful history.

What singled out this camp scene *long ago* is not so much the telling of tales or the sharing of staged activity. What *isolates* the experience in my mind are the varied effects of the colors I chose to illuminate the storytellers, all troubled children dutifully cared for at the Devereux Foundation.

Earlier, witnessing these fifty-seven boys and girls react disapprovingly to room colors imposed on them, I played a game with a rainbow of cards, exploring which part of the spectrum each one preferred. Keeping track of their responses, I continued the scenario during summer camp. While the

"I hate the color of that bedspread. Why did you choose that color?"
— *An 8-year old child at the Devereux Foundation, a residential treatment center*

"A child learns a lot about himself and his own individuality when he decides how his room looks and how it is arranged. The more input he has, the more likely he is to enjoy it, keep it orderly and show it off to friends as 'my room.'"
— *A Devereux counselor*

five- to twelve-year-olds took turns contriving pantomimes, I noted how positively every one always reacted when illuminated in their chosen color. At the same time, I observed how negatively they reacted when bathed in any other colored light.

Even more fascinating than this were their unanimous selections of specific colors if they were deficient in similar ways. For instance, children with speech problems were inclined towards green. Those with motor skill problems were predisposed towards red. Withdrawn children tended to seek out orange, while aggressive ones always picked blue. Learning-disabled children had a natural inclination towards purple.

Clearly, these young ones were favoring colors that most often related to their developmental needs, perhaps suggesting that certain body functions were supported by certain color choices.

What astonished me most about all of this was that it seemed just the opposite of what might be expected. Up to that point, my natural assumption would have been that active and aggressive children favor loud colors like red and orange and maybe yellow. Conversely, I would have thought that passive children feel most comfortable in calming colors like blues, greens and violets. Wasn't I surprised to discover quite the contrary!

Working later with twelve- to sixteen-year-olds in a state hospital setting, it impressed me how much color and light play such an important part in everyday life. Sheltered weekdays in sterile surroundings devoid of color and light, these severely brain-damaged wards of the state either wandered aimlessly or paced anxiously indoors as if sapped of energy or overcharged with it. Once outdoors absorbing the sun's rays and a natural environment, they were changed individuals, responding to activity and to daylight itself, not to mention all of nature's colors.

Even my red cap became a beacon of familiarity—not only because it signaled my weekly presence, but also because it stimulated them. That became evident the day a friend accompanied me wearing it. Amazingly, these mentally deficient children responded to the stranger just as they regularly responded to me. Obviously, it wasn't either of us that made the difference. It was that red cap.

Hoarding all this information in the recesses of my mind, I put my private theories about its meaning on hold when I moved to the West Coast. But even in an unrelated setting like a retail shop, thoughts about the importance of color surfaced time and time again. Involving myself in visual display work at Design Research, I began using color as a merchandising tool. Consciously incorporating bright goods in D/R's dark corners, I watched as shoppers now were drawn there. At inventory time, I perceived how much more merchandise remained to be sold in subdued colors than in bright ones. How powerful is the human response to color, I pondered, and how constant is its effect.

Ever fascinated by this subject, I ingested all the information I could find. The more I read, the more aware I became of how color has influenced humanity through the ages. From the eon of the cave man who drew crude markings with animal blood, to the era of the American Indian who painted his complexion with clay and mineral dyes, color has been a major influence in our lives.

Color's powers were so crucial to ancient

Merchandisers who recognize the human response to color are quick to incorporate certain colors in visual displays.

healing that our ancestors ages ago linked different shades with different ailments. While the Greeks used Tyrian purple from shellfish to remedy boils and ulcers, the Egyptians treated cataracts with green copper salt and other colored substances. Precious and semiprecious gemstones and the mystical properties they seemed to possess in their polished, light-reflective states also were revered to be medicinal. And the panacea of all kinds of ailments was thought to be prismatic diamond, the crystalline mineral whose chromatic brilliance is released in light.

My research on the subject uncovered other age-old beliefs tied to the symbolism of wearing certain colors. High courts reigned in royal blue and rich burgundy, while high priests divined in sacred purple robes. Clearly, color always has been the most recognizable way for man to define himself, his god, his country and his belongings. Perhaps that's why man has painstakingly spent centuries extracting nature's colors from plants and flowers and other living things.

COLOR AS LIGHT

But color isn't only the result of making dyes and mixing pigments. As the rainbow in the sky proves again and again, color is light reflected in particular wavelengths. As it appears in the spectrum, it spans red, orange, yellow, green, blue, indigo and violet, each flowing into the next. Component wavelengths of light produce the sensation of prismatic colors in the eye by stimulating the retina. Through a series of reactions, the photoreceptor cell of the eye passes the information to the brain. Along the way, the body itself is affected from the spine to the pituitary gland, which depends on light for growth and development.

As our energy-connected tissue matter is bombarded with waves of light, those organs that are molecularly sympathetic with the wavelength vibrating toward it will, in fact, absorb it, simply and easily. The exception to this rule is the damaged body. If a child is deaf, for instance, the wavelength of light commonly absorbed by the body's audio apparatus now finds great difficulty in its normal pathway. But surely, like the masterpiece that it is, always seeking the optimum situation for survival, the damaged body must compensate in some way for this lack of light to a certain area. Early in my research, I wondered if this could be why the children with similar afflictions I'd observed at Devereux always chose similar colors? Perhaps science would bear this out. . . .

NEWTON'S GENIUS

Prismatic properties of light were demonstrated first in 1666 by English philosopher and mathematician Sir Isaac Newton, the genius best known for formulating the laws of gravity, motion and calculus. Allowing a fine beam of sunlight entering a round hole in a shutter to pass through a glass prism and fall onto a screen, Newton produced the phenomenon of a rainbow array of colors that always had been explained as the latent color existing in the prism glass. By passing his miniature rainbow through another prism, however, Newton showed that the original white beam of light could be reconstituted since the colored lights recombined into white. Going a step further, he also illustrated that if a single color were selected from what he called the spectrum, nothing would alter it or break down its characteristics any further. Thus, Newton was led to the correct deduction that color is in light, not in glass, and that white light is actually a compound of all the colors in a spectrum.

Whether man perceives it that way or not, all color is light, and all light possesses color. The painted image on a cave wall, like the pigment in a royal robe, is nothing more than a select wavelength of reflected light by which the object is viewed after incident light falls upon it. The color we associate with specific objects depends entirely on what happens to the light that strikes it. As scientists have proven time and time again, colors are sensations resulting from light of different wavelengths reaching the eye. As long as objects are viewed in "white" light containing all wavelengths of the spectrum, they will appear to be the color most often associated with them. But should the wavelength distribution of incident light striking the objects vary so that certain frequencies are lacking, they will appear to be completely different colors. This happens much like a

LIGHT'S COLOR PROPERTIES

Not until Albert Einstein proved earlier in this century that energy and matter were the same, could man fully understand how all the world's objects interact with light to separate colors. Moving in waves like the ripples of a stream, light is a form of electromagnetic radiation with vibrations of electric and magnetic forces. In this fashion, it behaves like energy. Whenever light interacts with matter, as lamp emissions or substance absorption, it behaves as a form of matter composed of infinitesimal particles of electromagnetic energy called photons.

Light's color properties depend on its behavior as particles and as waves. Sometimes, light is absorbed by an object because certain of its photons are captured by the object's molecules. In fact, different molecules attract different colored photons. Leaves are good examples of how this works. The chlorophyll in them captures red light photons but not green photons, which bounce back out, providing the green light that gives them their color.

Simply put, the different colors of light represent photons of different energy. Violet and blue photons, which scatter more easily when they strike atmospheric dust and vapor, have nearly twice the energy of red, orange and yellow photons, which pass through the earth's atmosphere most readily. That is why the sky looks blue in daylight. Although the ocean is transparent, it, too, has a bluish color because it reflects the color of the sky.

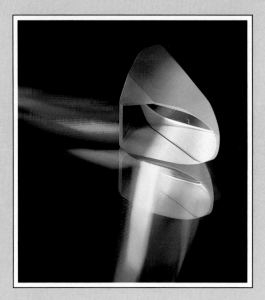

As scientists have proven time and time again, when light strikes a surface like a prism, its color properties are unleashed. The best example of this is the rainbow in the sky.

camera filter changes the color of objects seen through it.

By bending each color to a different degree, a prism separates the colors of light. Yet there are other ways to separate the spectrum's components. When light strikes a surface, some of the colors may be absorbed by the surface itself, enabling us to see only the colors that surface reflects. Consider snow, which reflects all colors of incident light but which the eye perceives as pure white. Our vision also tells us that bananas are yellow, but in actuality a banana reflects mainly yellow light, absorbing most other colors. What makes it look yellow is the color of light that reaches our eyes.

EMOTIONAL MEANING

But color's meaning in our lives is more than scientific. It's emotional, too, which is why individually we react positively and negatively to certain parts of the spectrum. For some people, red is reassuring, while for others, it is most discomforting. Sick people are calmed by blue, while well people are often chilled by it. Obviously, we realize color's impact, otherwise we wouldn't describe our feelings, well, so colorfully. When we are happy, we tell the world we're "in the pink." If we are sad, we're "feeling blue." If jealousy creeps into our emotions, we are "green with envy." Or if we are feeling cowardly, we admit to being "yellow bellied."

No less is the need for a child to experience the world as colorfully as he or she deems fit.

THE BODY PRISM

So far, we have concentrated on light and its colors as perceived through the eye. But as previously noted, the body also absorbs color through the skin when light literally bounces off it, interacting with the energy inherent in our makeup. Just like any other object suddenly illuminated, the body bends natural and man-made light while receiving it, channeling it through the system en route to the brain. Witness the sunbather soaking up sun rays. If too much light is absorbed at once, a sunburn results, affecting the parts exposed to the elements.

In everyday situations, the skin acts like a prism, breaking up white light into visible colors, allowing their absorption in different parts of the body. Every *body prism*, that is every human anatomy, responds to light in a different way. A ten-year-old Seattle boy inclined towards blue might choose a different color if he were living in Philadelphia. What matters is selecting that part of the spectrum which fulfills his personal needs at that time and place.

KIRLIAN'S CONTRIBUTION

Perhaps the first to isolate the colors relating to specific body functions was Soviet

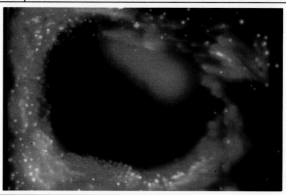

A Kirlian photo of an undamaged fingertip (above) shows its blue corona discharge. Witness the change in color (right) when the same fingertip is pricked with a needle.

electronic technician Semyon Kirlian. Working with his wife, Valentina, in the 1940s, he captured on photographic plates colored images of the energy emanating from life-forms undergoing physiological or emotional changes. The process referred to as Kirlian photography involves high-voltage electrical charges released at very low amperage through objects that radiate certain colors, or wavelengths, when photographed. Referred to as corona discharges, these colors sometimes appeared as halos around the substance being charged.

Devoting a decade to developing instruments that accurately measured this information, the Kirlians observed humans, plants, animals, and inanimate matter under exacting conditions. Quite by accident, the first object they scrutinized was Kirlian's own hand, burned in the process of trying to photograph tiny flashes of light from equipment normally used to administer electrotherapy to patients. The setting was a research institute where they were working. Holding a photographic plate in his hand under an electrode, Kirlian affected not only a burn but a strange imprint on the photo plate best described as a kind of luminescence shaped like the contours of his fingers. The image he recorded showed the colors being emitted from his singed fingertips at the moment of burning. Among other things, what this proved was the skin's absorption of light in much the same way as Newton's prism bent light.

By 1950, the Kirlians' photography had attracted scientific specialists throughout the world, from botanists to biologists to physicians.

The most fascinating findings the Kirlians made revolved around the areas of the body that received specific wavelengths of color as light. Their discovery led me to deduce the following:

- Red is absorbed in the base of the spine.
- Orange corresponds with the circulatory system.
- Yellow deals with the chest and lungs.
- Green relates to the throat.
- Blue corresponds to the eyes, ears and nose.
- Violet, absorbed on top of the head, corresponds to brain activities.

Interestingly, as their work evolved, the Kirlians uncovered more of the body's color mystery, this time dealing with damaged organs. What I ascertained was an association between such organs and the wavelengths of light normally absorbed by them. When someone was deficient in a certain area, the appropriate wavelength of light in that area was either diminished or missing. Just as I had discovered by chance at Devereux, and later intentionally with a child's color game, subjects share affinity for the same colors if they are deficient in the same way.

Using his methods, Kirlian photographed metals and living matter, obtaining unusual color arrangements under different conditions. The question that remains even today is: What exactly were his images representing? Moisture? Tem-perature? Electromagnetic energy? Or was it the release of moving body fluids creating vibrations as they journeyed through veins and arteries?

COLOR PERCEPTION

While science ponders answers to these questions, there are other color theories to contemplate.

When a baby is born, he can distinguish only black, white and gray. Within a week's time, he sees his first color, which is red. Because the infant will reach out for that color object, he will start to develop those perception skills. For this reason alone, baby girls in pink nurseries may develop at a quicker pace than baby boys in blue nurseries since the human eye sees pink before blue. Better to surround the newborn in delicate flesh tones than bright primary colors, which confuse a wee one's sensory skills, overwhelming him or her in the process.

Choosing a color, as I stated in an earlier chapter, is like choosing a radio station. While driving in a car, you may tune the dial to jazz or classical music or whatever suits you at the time. You choose color as light in much the same way, picking a part of the spectrum most appropriate for that moment.

How loud or soft you adjust the radio's volume is comparable to how bright or muted your color choice may be. In the case of a child picking the palette for his or her room, it's important to allow a sponta-

Given the chance to choose colors spontaneously, children will select that part of the spectrum that fulfills a personal need. The young ones responsible for the palettes here ranged from a toddler, who opted for light lavender, to a preschooler who chose cherry red. The green and blue rooms belong to two preteens.

neous response to that color game question: "If you could have one color card, which card will it be?" Each individual child, as each individual adult, selects the best situation to survive when given the opportunity to choose those things they really need and not just like. With color, it is very easy to make a choice based on outside influences such as a decorating magazine. But if you take time with a child, allowing for the child's spontaneous color selection, that color choice will be significantly true to his or her particular needs.

A word of caution to parents who undertake this exercise. Because a child chooses a specific color, do not make the mistake of thinking it necessarily corresponds to a damaged body area. Instead, it may relate to a body area that is simply developing in its own natural time frame.

One other word of advice to caregivers intent on making their charges happy. Often the desired effect of a color stimulus can be achieved in a simple area. A bulletin board covered in a fabric of the selected color will serve to supply the desired result. There's no need to bombard an environment in all directions with that color. This is where implementing the Master Plan coloring sketch takes its greatest role, hence, the reason for having your child color the sketch first with the crayons that correspond to the card choices made. Once those colors are used completely to the child's satisfaction, the rest of the drawing should be finished with the remainder of the crayons in the box, removing the initial ones from sight. Then, let the young one affecting these changes zero in on the exact intensity of the color picked by providing paint chips in that family, ranging from light to dark. Almost like that radio station turned up or down, the child will perceive how "loud" or "soft" his or her choice should be. By opening this doorway of expression, you encourage a positive self-image while satisfying a survival need.

Just as we outgrow clothes and habits, so, too, can we outgrow color at any age. The same child who elects the color blue at five may or may not opt for it at fifteen. Either situation is very natural and should never be forced. What's important here is the knowledge that whatever color the child chooses should be incorporated to some extent in his surroundings. A simple can of

Cotton-candy pink carpeting and a bulletin board define these quarters. Along the far wall, mirrored sliding closet doors reflect this collector's tiny treasures.

SEEING THE WORLD THROUGH COLOR-BLIND EYES

Not all people perceive colors in the same way, which is why colors probably don't all look the same to people with normal color vision. But a small percentage of the world's populace view life in what most of us would consider a crazy mixed-up spectrum.

Those who suffer from what we describe as color "blindness" are unable to distinguish between certain colors, although they do see the world in color. Where the normal eye sees the blue of the sky, the color-blind eye may see a sky of green or another color entirely.

People with defective color vision are thought to lack, or have reduced concentration, of one, two or all three of the cone cells that serve as the eye's color receptors. Those who confuse red and orange with yellow and green are called protanopes, while those who confuse green and yellow with orange and red, and cannot distinguish gray from purple, are called deuteranopes. Yet another group, tritanopes, confuse green with blue, and gray with violet or yellow.

Although children may be color blind, perceiving colors differently through their eyes than their peers, their faulty perception doesn't diminish their need for the color they select spontaneously to be part of their environment. Nor does their color vision impairment hamper the way they absorb color through their skin. Because we all receive colors through our skin, as the Kirlians and others demonstrated, even the blind experience color to a certain degree.

paint or a piece of fabric can profoundly change a young one's outlook.

As easy as this concept of color choice may seem, it is imperative to understand that it is not simply a matter of reversing these theories to achieve a desired result. Filling an environment with green, for example, may not encourage language skills. Or flooding a room with the color blue may not improve sight or hearing.

Color cannot be prescribed as if it were a bottle of blue or a gram of green. Each individual body prism receives and responds to color as light in its own unique way. All the more reason to ask a child to choose his or her own color preference.

HEALING POWERS

The therapeutic effects of color are just as important in the twentieth century as they were in the days of our distant ancestors. Even today, the basis for much medical diagnosis are the colors of different parts of the anatomy, from the eyes to the tongue to the skin to the body's secretions. Redness in the eyes sometimes relates to alcoholism . . . bluish purple skin indicates oxygen-deficient blood possibly stemming from lung or heart disease . . . bright red skin hints at carbon monoxide poisoning.

Even more precise in its color analysis is modern man's medical instrumentation such as infrared thermographs which register on a television monitor the infrared energy radiated by all matter. Mapping body temperature distribution, thermographs employ an infrared-sensitive scanning camera, detecting radiations color-coded as to intensity. An extraordinary instrument, it can detect some cancers early on as well as determine the fit of artificial limbs.

FULL-SPECTRUM LIGHT

Color's healing powers are packaged in other ways, too. The yellow beryl that ancients used as a jaundice curative and the green copper salt they utilized for cataracts have both been replaced by "blue light" treatment. Today, babies born prematurely with a jaundice condition no longer need blood transfusions. Now, excess bilirubin that the immature liver cannot remove is destroyed by blue light penetrating the skin over just a few days. What makes the blue light so medicinal is its ultraviolet property, which normally does not exist in incandescent or fluorescent bulbs. Since these common bulbs only supply five of

A regular dose of full-spectrum light enables premature infants to overcome jaundice in a matter of days.

the six wavelengths of light, they deprive man of one important element natural sunlight provides, namely ultraviolet.

When man first roamed the earth and made his home outdoors, he thrived in an environment where sun provided all wavelengths of light. When man moved indoors to windowed structures that prevented some of that natural sunlight from reaching his body, he deprived himself specifically of ultraviolet, a necessary ingredient for proper development. That is why it is so important to spend time on a regular basis not only outdoors absorbing some ultraviolet, but also indoors under lighting that contains these rays. Called blue or full-spectrum lights, they are an issue that a later chapter will explore in detail.

For now, suffice it to say that full-spectrum lighting is enabling health facilities to make strides in more than just nurseries. Surgery room staffs are witnessing more calming heart rates on the operating table

with patients who are flooded in full-spectrum light. I, too, have some success stories to tell about medical facilities that have allowed me to implement this kind of lighting in pediatric playroom and senior care design projects. For seniors, the full-spectrum light has allowed their cataract-inflicted eyes to see the contrasts between light and dark more clearly. Visual acuity particularly concerns this age group, who often have difficulty perceiving a piece of furniture from the floor covering below, or the landing from the rise in the staircase.

Creating a playroom for a pediatric hospital, I reinforced my theories about color's part in the healing process. Rather than supplying a single color in the room, I provided a half dozen primary and secondary colors, each placed in a distinctive area with corresponding floor tiles and wall markers. The activities assigned to those colors matched the body functions most often affected by those colors. It was not surprising to me when my follow-up observation revealed that children with specific ailments sought out the color area that cor-

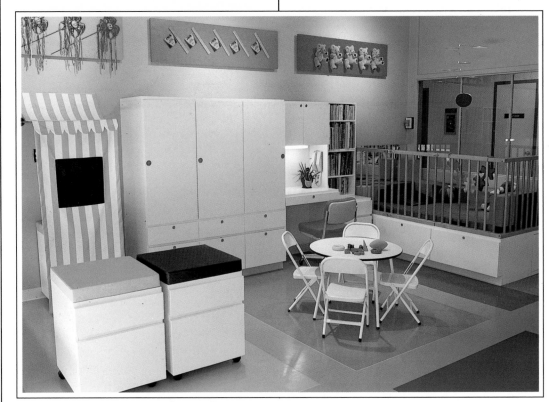

In a playroom at Children's Hospital in San Francisco activity areas vary in color scheme, correlating with specific development skills.

Sight- and hearing-impaired children in this hospital setting find comfort in this blue area during recuperation.

In this pediatric playroom, patients with mending muscles may feel invigorated by the color red.

related with their ailment. In other words, children with sore throats spent time in the green area. Children with broken limbs or mending muscles opted for the space done in red. Besides the restorative effect of colors in this hospital environment, what also contributed to the young patients' healing were the use of full-spectrum lights. As postoccupancy evaluation showed, the length of hospital stays decreased by a considerable percentage after the renovation.

To realize adequately the importance of ultraviolet light in our lives, judge the effects of those temporarily trapped in settings deprived of the sun's rays. Witness those confined to submarine duty or geographical areas with long, dark winters. Over a period of time, they suffer not only depression but certain physical afflictions including problems with bone and teeth development. Simple cure-alls for these groups and others thrust into light-deficient environments are the use of color and full-spectrum lighting.

Dancing teddy bears motivate those with broken limbs.

Whether confined to home or hospital, exercise is important. Slanted surfaces, movable block forms and large balls stimulate such activity.

THE SECRETS OF LIFE

Were it not for the movie *Cinderella*, one of this century's most incredible discoveries might never have been made; namely, that color and light play a crucial part in the life cycle.

Sparked by witnessing the cinematic transformation of a pumpkin into Cinderella's coach by means of animation, film genius Walt Disney envisioned an entire production devoted to plants and flowers growing from sprout to maturity in a matter of seconds through the miracle of time-lapse photography. Prevailing upon John Nash Ott, the pioneer cameraman behind this speeded-up photographic process, Disney plotted his classic *Secrets of Life* to catalog the evolution of pumpkins, apples and other vegetation.

Down in the basement studio he called his "ivory tower," Ott immediately stumbled upon a problem with startling scientific significance. Planting the pumpkin fruit under a skylight, he supplemented restricted natural daylight (and approximated full summer sun intensity) with "cool white" fluorescent lights. Although the vines grew, all of their female, or pistillate-producing flowers, turned brown, dropping off soon after their formation. Meanwhile, the male pollen-producing flowers, the staminate, grew vigorously but were useless all by themselves on this monoecious plant which bears both reproductive organs.

Delayed a whole year by the growing season into trying his luck at photobiology again, Ott replaced his flickering old fluorescent fixtures with new "daylight-white" tubes. To his utter amazement, the next time around the exact opposite happened: all the pistillate buds developed fully while the staminate buds dropped off! In both cases, the vines had been photographed for months every five minutes, from the time seeds were planted to a growth over fifteen feet.

Upon researching the differences in the two experiments, Ott concluded that two light sources affected the two results. Cool-white fluorescents, the kind used initially, are strong in the yellow/orange part of the color spectrum. On the other hand, daylight-white fluorescents, the kind in the second test, have more blue in them.

Ott's discovery that either male or female flowers could be cultivated by controlling slight variations in color, or wavelength of light, posed some interesting implications for more than just pumpkins. It also instilled an insatiable thirst in Ott for more information on the effects of color and light on living things. Since that first surprise in his basement laboratory back in the 1950s, Ott has devoted decades to this subject's study, eventually establishing the Environmental Health and Light Research Institute.

Working first with plant life, then later with animal and human life, Ott uncovered over and over again the ill effects of fluorescent lighting on whatever life-form it was illuminating. Comparing it to natural sunlight, he realized that the prime

Full-spectrum Light

Fluorescent Light

Incandescent Light

element missing in artificial lighting was ultraviolet, a ray beyond the visible spectrum, prevented further from entering our indoor worlds by standard window glass, which reflects it. With that in mind, Ott approached leading manufacturers, eventually convincing the Duro-Test Company to produce a full-spectrum fluorescent tube to duplicate as nearly as possible the natural spectrum of outdoor sunlight. Called Vita Lite, the product Ott consulted on is a patented general-purpose fluorescent tube that simulates the full color and beneficial ultraviolet spectrum of sunlight. An all-purpose white light, it enables those illuminated by it to see black and white more distinctly and sharply than under ordinary fluorescents, not to mention colors and details in a truer and more accurate form.

Through the decades, Ott has done some remarkable experimentation, discovering the effects of color and light on myriad living things. Among the most noteworthy are the following:

Fluorescent lighting:
- May trigger hypertension, headaches and insomnia.
- May cause fatigue, malaise and hyperkinesis in children.
- May decrease the rate of calcium absorption essential for maintaining the body's bones, teeth and muscle tone.

Full-spectrum lighting:
- Increases the rate of intestinal calcium absorption necessary for proper bone metabolism, which otherwise only occurs under sunlight exposure, probably because of vitamin D synthesis.
- Increases productivity, improves health and fosters better mental attitudes.
- Retards the incidence of arthritis.
- Has remarkable curative effects on skin cancers, near-blindness, goiter and arthritis.

Additionally, Ott revealed that by preventing ultraviolet rays from entering the nervous system through the eye, as nature originally intended, even certain sunglasses and contact lenses may be detrimental to health, provoking illness and eye disease. Moreover, he detected harmful effects not only from fluorescents but from everyday objects such as digital watches, color televisions, smoke detectors, and video display terminals, which not only may weaken muscles but also may diminish sex drive.

Although scoffed by some, Ott's research dealing with light's influence on plants, animals and humans has earned him much worldwide acclaim, including an honorary doctorate from Chicago's Loyola University and the Grand Honors Award of the National Eye Institute. His input also shaped the ideas of scientists designing the first United States space station.

Considering the scope of Ott's research, it's imperative to pay attention to the lighting surrounding us from the classroom to the lunchroom to the sick room. As Ott so aptly expresses it in one of his books: "Light is a nutrient much like food— the wrong kind can make us ill and the right kind can help keep us well."

A VITAL ROLE

From "Suite Allison" to hospitals today, I'm convinced that color plays a vital role in our well-being and overall health. A brief look at some of the young clients I've had through the years underscores this conviction.

- A young boy, hearing-impaired since birth, chose a deep blue for his living and learning environment, creating a positive place to sleep and play. This color added greatly to supporting his skills and strengthening his weaknesses.

- A playful preteen with a full athletic life retreated from the loud orange and yellow he was so familiar with as an infant, to quiet turquoise blues. The new haven became the one place in this young man's life where he could be very peaceful.

- A hyperactive twelve-year-old boy, brain damaged since birth, wanted a retreat "more grown up" than the childish place he called his own, with its earth-tone decor and natural wood furnishings. Choosing purple to color his world, he fashioned a contemplative space for a previously tense, nervous individual. By applying his choice to bedcovers, desktop and curtains, the room was filled with mindful color.

To comprehend fully the importance of a child's choice of the palette that will color his room, remember that certain colors may relate to certain parts of the body. As my research has explored time and time again,

Communication skills thrive in this green activity area where audio-visual equipment is concentrated.

Part of the healing process for young patients involves playing with colors and fingerpaints.

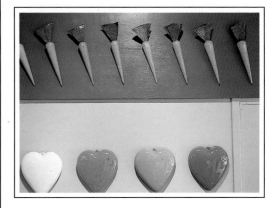

Decorative carrot and heart displays help hospitalized children foster fantasy play.

Color and light join forces in the pediatric solarium at Children's Hospital in San Francisco. Located adjacent to the playroom pictured throughout this chapter, the glassed-in social setting enables young ones on the mend to stretch out on a large floor surface or curl up on a sunny window seat.

the colors children pick spontaneously as their preference correspond to a physical part of the anatomy that either may be developing or deficient in a skill particular to that area. A boy learning a second language is apt to choose green, the same color the boy with a speech problem might choose. Clearly, both conditions deal with vocal skills.

BODY COLORS

In my experience, it has become apparent that colors and their corresponding body functions include the following:

● RED: Concerns itself with the base of the spine and consequently motor skill activities. A color that raises the blood pressure and increases respiration, red gets the metabolism going—the arms, legs and any gross motor activity using the limbs. This is the last color children experience when they leave the womb, and the first color they identify in this world.

● ORANGE: Corresponds to circulation and nervous systems. Orange has a tremendous tonic effect. When you have a cold and try to combat infection, somehow you crave the color of orange juice as well as the nutrient of vitamin C.

● YELLOW: Responds to the chest, heart and lungs. The functions affected by yellow appear to be respiration and cardiopulmonary activity. Children with asthma and other breathing problems react most favorably to yellow. Perhaps this gives new meaning to the phrase "heart of gold."

● GREEN: Relates to the throat and vocal cords. This affects developing speech skills. Children learning a second language will tend to choose green, as will children with speech impediments. Mother Nature's most predominant color is considered the most restful to the eye. Throughout history, it also has been associated with vigorous growth.

● BLUE: Correlates to eyes, ears and nose, which involve seeing, hearing and smelling. Sight- and hearing-impaired children are inclined to favor blue. My observations have shown that the more severely hearing-impaired a child is, the deeper the color blue chosen. A cool color, blue has a calming effect on the heart rate and respiratory system.

● VIOLET: Corresponds to the top of the head and cerebral activity. A color supporting nonverbal activity, it often is represented in religious paintings as the saintly hue of halos. Heads of state and heads of church wear purple or reddish purple burgundy to symbolize high levels of wisdom and authority. In children, it may signify a young mind deep in thought, concerned or even afraid about something that's confusing.

Although they do not relate to any specific parts of the body, several other color choices need some clarification.

● EARTH TONES: All ground colors—gray, beige, brown—and animal tones—fawn, squirrel, dove—do what they purport to do. They ground you. They do not elevate the blood pressure or slow it down. They essentially make you sedentary.

● BLACK: As the absence of all light, black is therefore the absence of all color. It is darkness at its maximum level. If a child favors black as a room color, the reason could be avoidance of some stimulus.

● WHITE: As the presence of all light, white is therefore the presence of all color. It is lightness at its maximum level. If a child can't decide what color to put in a room, then use white because it supplies the full spectrum as reflected light.

Although mentioned previously, it's worth repeating: Don't assume, because your child picks a certain color, that the child is alerting you to a corresponding body area that's damaged. The choice simply may relate to an area developing in its own natural way.

OUT ON A LIMB CHOOSING COLORS

If a roomful of grown-ups were given a chance to "pick a card" from any color of the rainbow, what color would most of them pick?

That special challenge was mine to undertake in 1981 when the public at large lit an electronic Christmas tree in the colors they favored.

Red. Orange. Yellow. Green. Blue. Violet. Those were the push-button choices spectators had to illuminate a thirty-foot silvertip pine that served as the centerpiece for San Francisco's Elegant Celebration of Christmas.

Devised by me with expertise from computer technologists at California-based Atari Corporation, the one-of-a-kind rainbow tree was engineered so that hundreds of lights in all six colors of the spectrum popped on as people depressed buttons at computer stalls in front of them. As they made their personal choices, they were bathed in that color—as was the toy-laden tree from the base to the tip. When the lights reached the star at the top, "We Wish You A Merry Christmas" automatically played. Once they lifted their hands, the lights turned off.

During the annual fundraiser, individual responses were tallied electronically daily. Of the 110,000 plays recorded, 65,000 (roughly two-thirds), chose the color purple. What was interesting to me was that the control station for purple deliberately was placed behind the tree, out of immediate view.

Conversely, the button in closest proximity was red, the color many speculated would be favored. Ironically, it was chosen least, perhaps because the building's interior was predominantly brick red, therefore supplying more red than each observer needed.

I wanted to know if purple would be sought out intentionally, since weeks earlier I predicted that purple would be the most preferable. What prompted me to conclude that, even before the first button was pushed, was the belief that purple is a cerebral color, supporting nonverbal activity. In my estimation, the mental questions the selectors would ask themselves (such as "What is my choice?" and "Where is it located?") would precipitate their thought processes.

The crowd's choice of the color purple was reinforced later that season when the tree was resurrected in its entirety at San Francisco's City Hall rotunda. For the two weeks that it stood there, accepting human touches to control its illumination, there were 60,000 color choices made by the public. More than half once again chose the color purple!

As this specially devised electronic Christmas tree suggests, color choice may depend more on the effects of surroundings than personal taste.

FROM THE EYES OF BABES

Nowhere is the powerful influence of color more evident than through the eyes of our children.

Each perceptive moment of their early years latches on to the spectrum. As touch, taste, smell and sound deeply mold the child's abilities, so, too, does color become an integral part of the whole child.

The soft inviting tones of a mother's flesh . . : the multicolors of bedcovers . . . the wall treatment . . . clothing . . . the quality of light that enters their world. Each of these is absorbed, recorded and recalled again and again throughout life.

As much care and concern that is given to feeding, nurturing and loving our children should be given to the quality of color and light imposed on them during their for-·mative years.

CHAPTER 4

Room to Grow

> *"It felt like it was me—like I had something to say and that what I said about my room went. If I wanted something to happen, it would happen. It was great!"*
> —Allison at fourteen

> *"It taught her a fervor for life, a zest for ideas and a joy in color and spirit and adventure. It was a great addition to her life."*
> —Allison's mother, Barbara

To Allison's parents, their daughter's empty milk-white room looked blank and bare the day they moved to a different address.

But to Allison and me, this corner of her family's new everyday world seemed like an artist's clean canvas, awaiting colorful strokes.

As the child dreamed aloud of the way her quarters should someday look, I wondered how different they would be from the make-believe setting she co-designed just eight weeks earlier for the San Francisco Decorator Showcase.

Stretching across the walls in her home surroundings, she informed me, should be a rainbow whose pastel rays fanned at the midway point. Spilling over her bed should be cotton candy striped sheets, containing every color of the spectrum. Rocks and shells would keep constant company with toy dinosaurs and dolls, not to mention a team of stuffed animals and a real dog named Sophie.

Listening intently to this six-year-old's fantasies was not just idle exercise. Magazine editors at *Better Homes and Gardens* had presented me with a mighty challenge, anxious to show their millions of readers new ways to think about decorating for children. Could I prove on the pages of their publication my theory that children's rooms needn't become outmoded as time passes? Simply stated, the concept means that young ones shouldn't have to outgrow their personal environment as they do their clothes. Instead, fill their domain with adaptable furnishings that allow for convertibility and meet their needs for years to come.

A TEST IN TRANSITION

Using Allison as a prime candidate and her new home as a perfect setting, I proposed to equip a six-year-old's room so it could function ten years later as a teen retreat with nearly all the same furnishings. For practicality, I promised spending no more than an additional $300 on the transition.

Though eager to begin translating her young ideas into workable surroundings, I put that part of the project on hold. Since the room eventually would be Allison's (at age six), it made more sense to design the sixteen-year-old's setting first, then replace it with the one that would last. But for a better understanding of how the process normally develops, let's reverse the six-to-sixteen-year-old design project as Allison experienced it, so it falls into typical chronological order.

An intelligent child, Allison realized from the start that the showcase suite named in her honor never was meant to serve as her personal sleep chamber. Perhaps because it was just pretend, she didn't want her own room to resemble it very much except for the closet loft. "I guess I didn't want a room just done," she explains today. "I kind of wanted to do it myself."

And do it she did by spinning little girl dreams of rainbow walls and striped sheets and funny fabric dinosaurs. "It felt like it was me," she says looking back. "Like I had something to say and that if I wanted something to happen, it would happen. It was great!"

In Allison's first-grade opinion, "great" meant arranging everything just so in a

Convertibility plays a key role in this 6-year-old's setting. Every component, from rolling cart to retractable lighting, functions well for the same child years later.

Measuring cups and other simple gadgetry create this mathematical learning area.

room that measured eleven by fourteen feet.

• The comforter-covered striped twin bedding became a cozy corner unit. Instead of being placed on a frame, it was stacked on a sturdy piece of plywood, then elevated on white plastic storage cylinders. They were perfect for holding toys and other tiny treasures and for supporting a young sleeper.

• Most of the learning centers functioned as organized modular shelf sections, stretching along each wall as surfaces to work on from child-size chairs. Others served as special interest areas, like a ballerina bar before a wall mirror, or a budding artist's clipboard on the back of the connecting bathroom door.

• Even the lighting was child level, suspended on retractable cords. Crisscrossed on tracks in an "X" formation, the four round ceiling-mounted metal fixtures were a chalk-white factory-type design. Their height was adjustable.

• Bright rubber-backed rugs of the bathroom variety were scattered about the room. That way a child could move from one to another wherever play was suitable.

• A rolling storage cart, like the kind artists sometimes use, was an added touch. Its slide-out trays secured all sorts of treasures, from dolls and jump rope to crayons and craft paper.

• Candy-striped Roman shades allowed a little girl privacy from the outside world. When she wanted to peek

Fluffy floor mats permit many resting places.

beyond her realm, she climbed on the bed to reach the pull cords.

"I had everything, everything I needed," Allison reflects wistfully, admitting she spent quite a bit more time in the space after its transformation than before when she considered it "just a room."

For Allison, what made the difference between the showcase suite that she affected and her own habitat was the added freedom to start from scratch. "I had everything to do with my own room and it was exactly how I wanted it. What made it different the second time around, I think, was my touch," she says in retrospect.

A GROWN-UP GIRL'S SCENE

Yet no matter how much Allison loved those surroundings, sooner or later changing tastes and budding interests would require a revamp of the room's scenery. In just a short decade this spirited sprite probably would pursue more grown-up pleasures. How well she could do that with the same furnishings remained to be seen.

Giving Allison room to grow on the pages of a home decorating magazine was a week-long project launched with paint. Because a teen likely would want more space than a small child, the walls were coated white to create an atmosphere that looked larger than it actually was. A wide band of burgundy rimmed the room, equal to the height of the window top. Replacing the low wall stripes that kept a younger child

What once suited a 6-year-old has been transformed into a setting for someone 10 years older.

in scale to her surroundings, the burgundy band visually raised the ceiling to make a taller person feel more comfortable. So, too, were the other changes geared for a girl who had realized a growth spurt in mind and body.

• The teen's twin bed is no longer tucked in a cozy corner. Now center stage, it sports sleek bed linens in rich burgundy. The reverse design of the original bedcovering is a bold departure from little girl stripes. To add more sophistication, a shiny brass headboard completes the picture, previously devoid of any bed frame at all.

• Learning centers that once ringed the room now have a new personality. Stacked floor to ceiling along one wall, these modular units have assumed the identity of an entertainment center, storing books and belongings for nonstudy hours.

• The growing wardrobe of a high school student deserves more space than

Even a child's closet should reflect a growth in mind and body.

a first grader, so a closet loft has been converted to simple shelving and the clothes rod raised to accommodate longer fashions. The low triple-decker closet drawers that once stored a little girl's wardrobe accessories now sit by the window as sides of a desk topped with cut-to-fit particle board. Resting where the drawers were in the closet corner are the white cylindrical storage units that once formed the base of the six-year-old's bed. Now, they support a vanity which is adjacent to a rolling cart that used to contain toys and art supplies. But image is important now, so makeup and hair gear refortify the slide-out trays.

• A young adult doesn't need ceiling light as low as a child, so the four suspended fixtures have been retracted closer to the ceiling.

• The small scatter rugs that seemed just right in a six-year-old's room look out of place as the sole floor treatment in a room for someone ten years older. A larger area rug has been added in deep burgundy to carry out the color scheme and serve as a focal point. A few small throw rugs in neutral tones complete the look.

• To adapt to the needs of a teenage accumulator, more storage has surfaced in the older girl's room. In the form of wire shelving, it supports greenery outside the window. The supplies of a budding gardener rate equal treatment in wire shelves along the back of the connecting bathroom door where once a child's sketch pad hung. Still more storage is by

BABY SPACE

Nursery.

The very word conjures thoughts of newborns protectively cradled in whisper-soft surroundings.

Yet, look around at the nurseries in friends' and relatives' homes. More often than not, rooms set aside for infants are far from tranquil havens. Instead, reflecting the marketplace, they are ablaze with brash colors and bold designs. Cheery though they may be to the average adult, they hardly delight the one they were meant for, if scientific data is accurate. As hospital research shows, primary colors overwhelm babies, confusing their limited sensory skills.

While this book addresses needs of the postcrib set, a few thoughts follow on the subject of decorating a nursery, which in itself could cover book proportions.

When newborns open their eyes in this world, they see sights in white, gray and black. That's because infant retina rods and cones perceiving the spectrum have not matured enough to distinguish red, orange, yellow, green, blue and violet. By week's end, however, they already can detect red, yet they prefer looking at black and white objects that show dramatic contrast. Not for six to nine months will they outgrow this. With that in mind, it is far better to stimulate an infant visually with black-and-white geometric shapes like a mobile of checkerboards, bulls' eyes and stripes. To foster stimulation, change these hanging toys periodically or replace them with black-and-white photographs, preferably of Mom and Dad, whose faces babies recognize.

Because an infant reaches out when finally discerning the color red, he or she then starts developing depth perception skills. As mentioned previously, for this reason baby girls in pink nurseries may develop at a quicker pace than baby boys in blue nurseries since the human eye sees pink well before blue.

Flesh tones might be the better choice to color a newborn's first surroundings, avoiding juvenile-themed paraphernalia that deluge baby stores. Framed prints peppering the place can provide a touch of whimsy while you wait for the child to grow to the point where personal choices can be made.

Aside from the physical benefits simple uses of color and light will reap on a young one, this kind of room treatment lends itself to convertibility as time passes. Repainting the walls as baby grows is one quick, affordable way to accomplish a new look. So is acquiring various bedcovers.

Because of the rapidity with which a baby changes those first few years, it isn't as easy as it is with an older child to outfit a nursery with flexible furnishings. However, there are some options, such as multifunctional crib sets that can be reconfigured into storage bins, dressers and other necessary units. Even some contemporary changing tables convert to dressers for storage.

When a soft, cuddly newborn enters your world, it's only natural to want to shower affection in the form of creature comforts. But resist the urge to fill this environment with furnishings that won't serve beyond baby's first steps. Except for a crib, changing table and a few incidentals, better to hold off on major room purchases until the one occupying this space can derive both pleasure and value from picking the surroundings personally.

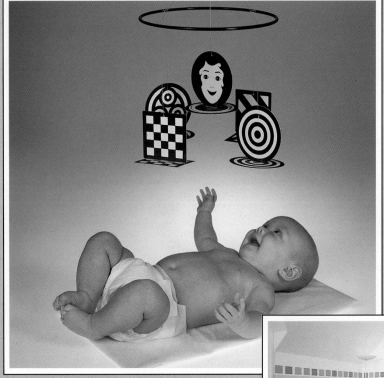

Black and white geometric designs and faces detail this Infant Stim-Mobile. Infants prefer this over more colorful stimuli during the first six to nine months while the rods and cones of vision are developing.

Buy only the basics, like a crib and changing table, if you're outfitting a nursery.

the bed where two cylinders originally housed under the child's sleep area now are out in the open. Their new duties as bedside tables provide support for telephone and houseplants.

● To lend a grown-up touch, striped Roman shades have been replaced with crisp white shutters like the kind that frame a home's exterior. Hung full length to the sides of the indoor picture window, they give the illusion of a larger opening and therefore lend a dramatic touch.

"It was a great room. I could have lived in it when I was six!" Allison says of the teen retreat. "I thought it was so big and mature," she continues, adding "but I didn't like it better than my very own room."

Allison's mother is the first to admit she was somewhat skeptical about the idea that furnishings in a child's room could function adequately into teenagehood. "But when I actually saw how easily it was done, it made so much sense. It was not only practical but a real possibility."

AN EYE TOWARD THE FUTURE

Creating a "room to grow" for your child is a lesson in long-term planning. Because youthful tastes change as quickly as youthful bodies, it's important to view purchases with an eye towards future use. Just as you wouldn't expect a five-year-old to fit into the fashions of a two-year-old, you shouldn't expect a five-year-old's personalized setting to be appropriate ten years later for the same individual.

But changing the scenery as a child matures doesn't have to mean changing the furnishings. As the transition of Allison's room from a first grader's quarters to a teenager's retreat proved to magazine readers, the trick to accomplishing this kind of conversion is shopping with flexibility in mind. Resist the urge to carry out an overall theme in a child's room by passing up whimsically related merchandise that time-locks the look. Long after a child has lost interest in a cartoon character, an item covered with its face will annoy the very person it was meant to amuse. Better to forgo decaled and spray-painted furnishings in favor of more basic designs that are tireless in appeal. Perhaps an ever-changing bulletin board or corkboard would be the proper place to display the object of a young fan's affection.

The key to finding adaptable pieces for growing children is scrutinizing potential buys, asking yourself how they will serve the needs of someone young a few years down the road. Don't let a sale price dictate a purchase that soon will be obsolete. Good investments early on far outweigh the process of repeat buying.

Before searching the marketplace for convertible pieces, make mental note of what features merit consideration. Besides durability, the best buys in children's furnishings have easy-to-clean surfaces sturdy enough to withstand playtime punishment.

Pink and blue squares stitched into this wall-to-wall green carpeting encourage motor skill activity.

High on my list of recommendations are well-made modular units that stack, allowing for different interpretations to accommodate a growing child. Remember the learning centers in six-year-old Allison's room? Clustered atop each other in the same setting she could occupy a decade later, they formed a wall unit that better met the needs of an active teenager.

Often, modular products that meet these requirements are made of mold-injected plastic in seamless shapes. Less likely to crack at the joints, they are ideal building blocks for growing bodies and expanding minds that like to flip and stack and rearrange the components of their world as needs and interests change. One advantage of such lightweight furniture is the ability for a child to alter effortlessly his or her surroundings.

Natural wood is another excellent choice for children's furnishings, especially if you're contemplating pieces custom-made for the room. My personal preference is wood. It not only brings the outdoors in, it instills an appreciation in young ones for

It's important for children to be able to see and reach certain treasures. This combination storage/bookcase unit provides such an option.

Modular stacking units invite reconfiguration. Topped with cushions, these inexpensive storage pieces double as window seating.

natural fibers. Top it or trim it in colorful laminate and make a more personalized statement that can be altered reasonably as someone matures. In much the same way that bedcovers can be reversible, wood furnishings can be devised with reversible laminate tops, providing a flexibility factor.

Just like modular plastic pieces, modular wood units invite reconfiguration. Stack open "boxes" and create tiered bookshelves. Or stack closed "boxes" and build a chest with myriad drawers. Bridge

"boxed" units with a board, and fashion a work station. The possibilities are limited only by imagination.

ALTERNATE SOURCES

Although furniture stores may carry modular furnishings, other sources might provide some interesting alternatives in the quest for convertible merchandise.

The following sources deserve investiga-

tion before deciding on final purchases.

● Building supply stores that sell unfinished wood products like simple particle board cubes.

● Hardware stores that carry molded rubber storage items well-suited for all kinds of uses.

● Department store lifestyle sections that show upscale home office furnishings.

● Scandinavian stores that promote unpretentious pieces following the tradition of "form follows function."

SHOPPING CHECKLIST

As you embark on your shopping expedition, make a checklist of the major items to consider as convertible furnishings best suited for children's rooms.

Stacked or used singly, cubes perform multiple functions.

● STACKING WOOD CUBES: Basic building blocks for growing bodies, these multifunctional units can serve as seating or storage containers or a combination of both. Stacking capabilities stretch their possible use from low storage containers to bookcases to desk components to bed supports. By enabling you to create systems of varying heights, simple cubes can help teach a child spatial relationships, motor skills and coordination as that child reaches different heights.

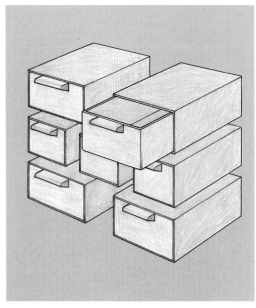

Plastic storage endures most childish spills.

● PLASTIC CONTAINERS: Often seen in adult settings as bathroom towel storage, molded plastic containers are waterproof, an excellent feature for furnishings likely to endure childish spills. Besides serving as receptacles for all kinds of treasures, they work well as side tables in a room for any age. Also stackable, they allow for many configurations.

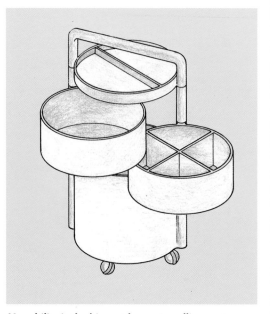

Movability is the biggest bonus to rolling carts.

● ROLLING CARTS: What makes movable furniture so functional is its ability to become a work or play space wherever whim or need dictate. Carts like those used by artists or beauticians have the added capability of storing possessions that hide from view with sliding doors.

Both chalkboard and pegboard play are possible with this custom unit containing built-in storage for chalk, erasers and pegs. Unlatched from its wall perch, it drops down to become the bed pictured on the next page.

Whether shared with a sibling or an overnight friend, extra bedding is important to consider in a child's room. Bunks, trundles and units like this custom one offer sleeptime solutions for more than one.

● BEDS: Realizing how often children like to share their space with an overnight friend, give serious thought to a trundle bed. Space savers that provide extra sleeping at a moment's notice, trundles function well as storage for pillows, blankets, clothing or toys. If space alongside a single bed is at a premium and your budget will permit, examine the possibility of a custom-built trundle that slides out somewhat like a drawer from the foot of the bed rather than the side, offering easy access to both sleeping and storage spaces while not requiring as much valuable floor space. Trundles made in this fashion also have the distinct advantage of allowing easier access to each sleeper than a side-by-side trundle permits.

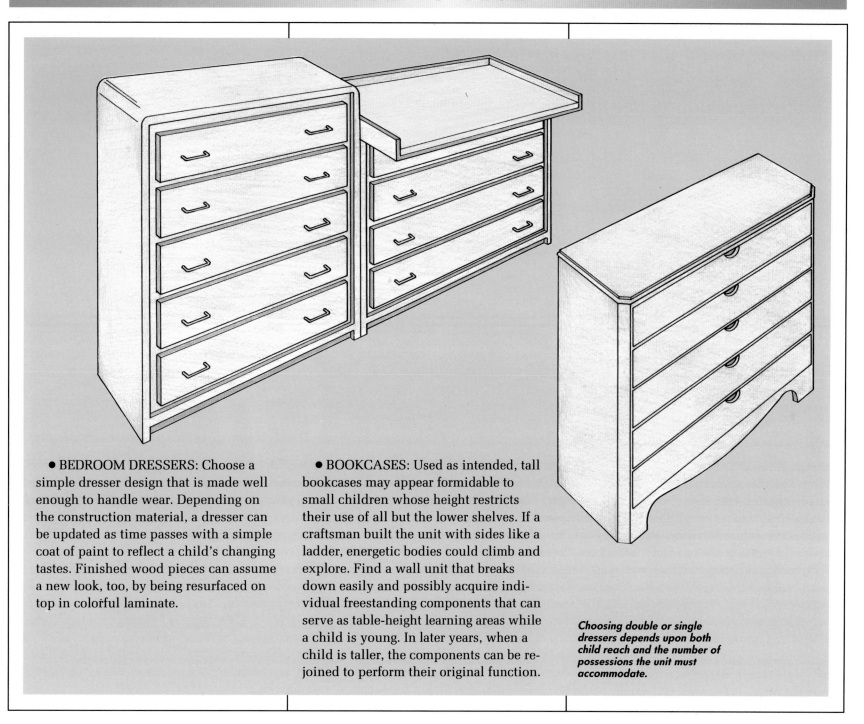

● BEDROOM DRESSERS: Choose a simple dresser design that is made well enough to handle wear. Depending on the construction material, a dresser can be updated as time passes with a simple coat of paint to reflect a child's changing tastes. Finished wood pieces can assume a new look, too, by being resurfaced on top in colorful laminate.

● BOOKCASES: Used as intended, tall bookcases may appear formidable to small children whose height restricts their use of all but the lower shelves. If a craftsman built the unit with sides like a ladder, energetic bodies could climb and explore. Find a wall unit that breaks down easily and possibly acquire individual freestanding components that can serve as table-height learning areas while a child is young. In later years, when a child is taller, the components can be rejoined to perform their original function.

Choosing double or single dressers depends upon both child reach and the number of possessions the unit must accommodate.

Bookcases that break down into separate components may become individual learning centers for the very young.

• DESKS: Open your mind to more than conventional desk systems and discover all kinds of options. Modular units, such as stacked open "boxes," can support plywood or a hollow core door that adequately serve as desktops. So, too, can a piece of laminate serve well atop tiers of plastic drawers or heavy-duty metal bins.

• CHAIRS: With adjustable seats and backs that allow for multiple positions, secretarial desk chairs with legs on casters are a good choice for growing bodies. Their adjustable heights easily accommodate six- to sixteen-year-olds.

As you examine would-be purchases, scrutinize the entire construction. Check safety features on all sides. Avoid storage chests with heavy lids that all too easily can fall on a child's head or hands. Open storage with shelves and bins is the safest, but check this, too, for rough or jutting edges that can bruise tender skin.

Hardware is another important consideration. Steer clear of furniture with large knobs since small fingers lack the strength and motor skills to pull them. By ignoring features like oversize knobs, you not only frustrate young ones but thwart their learning process. A better choice is a drawer pull that little hands can grasp.

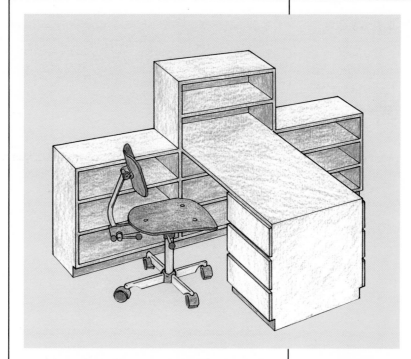

Desks with ample work surfaces are essential for projects.

For smaller children, stools provide not only lightweight seating but a step up to shelves otherwise out of reach.

BEYOND THE BASICS

Creating a space with built-in convertibility goes beyond buying furniture. For a room that really adapts to the young one living there, be mindful of other considerations.

● BED LINENS: Buy or make a reversible comforter or comforter covers with more sophisticated fabric on one side. As the child matures, flip the bedding to reflect a more adult personality. Bolster pillows on top of a bed also have convertibility features. They can serve ably as more than decoration by either propping players or board games or forming table surfaces for specific play activity.

● WALL DECOR: Whether clocks or artwork or other equipment, hang wall objects at the eye level of the one viewing them on a regular basis. Things towering overhead at adult height give the clear message that this is not a place for a child-size person.

● LIGHTING: Raise or lower the height of overhead lighting easily if you acquire illumination with retractable cords. This kind of system is especially effective for children who like to read on the floor, affording them good light at a low level.

If secured to the windowsill rather than the top of the window frame, the cords of Roman shades allow small hands to maneuver and adjust light exposure. Velcro tabs keep the fabric from spilling over.

● WINDOW COVERINGS: Be mindful that traditional window treatments geared for adults don't always serve the needs of children. Certain styles, like Roman shades or venetian blinds, should be hung so that small hands can maneuver the cords to adjust light exposure. This may mean securing some shades to the windowsill rather than to the top of the window frame while the child is very

By day, these bay window coverings pull up to allow light to filter through many panes. When night falls, they drop down for privacy and warmth. Black out curtains behind assist in blocking out unwanted light.

Metal mini blinds are a good option in a room where maximum light exposure is desired. Built-in window seats conceal toy storage.

young. In that case, use Velcro tabs to keep the fabric from spilling over the window. When the child's growth spurt allows for handling cords at a higher level, change shade position to the standard location. Other window options lending themselves to convertibility include mini blinds, available with a different color on either side. By simply reversing the direction of the blades, a new color scheme can be achieved.

● WALLS: As a child's frame stretches toward adulthood, so, too, can the visual height of his room by just raising the

Drawing paper hung from a clipboard turns this door into an artistic center for a creative child.

paint border that encircles it. Called a dado, this line or decorative detail should be at a child's head height, keeping that child in proportion to the room.

• DOORS: Even the back of a door can serve as a work or activity center with a hanging clipboard or craft paper holder. This might also be the perfect location for certain storage pouches, such as fabric shoe pockets that work well as containers for dolls and whatnot. As the child matures, the same spot may accommodate more grown-up equipment like a large plastic grid system or a wire shelf rack to house paraphernalia.

CLOSET ENCOUNTERS

But a room's most convertible factor might be out of ordinary view. None other than the closet, it contains the element of flexibility, key to this entire concept. Devoid of doors, flooded with light and filled with color, the closet can function as auxiliary space for work and play besides storage. As someone with fond childhood memories of moments tucked away in a built-in wardrobe, I know well the joy a young one derives from such a bedroom retreat.

Since very young children require very little space to keep their small clothes, the closet is an ideal place to incorporate a hideaway loft in lieu of an upper shelf. Accessible by means of a built-in ladder, the loft could include a custom cushion, serv-

ing as a special place to nap behind a safety bar. This on-high haven could also be a lookout or a private refuge to visit when it's time to be left alone.

But lofty perches are far from the only possibilities closet transformations can provide.

Why not:

• Convert a closet into a puppet theatre by hanging a piece of custom-slit fabric where the door would be?

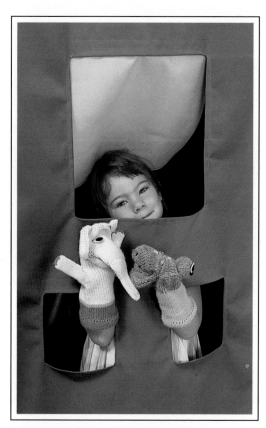

Cloth characters come to life with this puppet stage hung in place of a closet door.

• Create a makeup alcove for a budding young girl who likes to fuss with her appearance?

• Separate quiet time from fast play periods by placing the bed in a large walk-in closet?

• Devise two distinct areas by dividing a closet in half with a wall, assigning clothes storage to one side and toy storage to the other?

Even closets kept in their original state can assume a dual personality by adding varied rods and hooks to redefine the territory. Simple strips of wood spaced evenly to line every inch of wall make orderly storage a snap with holders that hook onto each rung.

As new heights of the person inspiring these changes require more space for hanging clothes, remove childish traces like sleeping lofts and special ladders and puppet theatres. In their place you might consider more grown-up features such as storage containers or built-in cubicles to house sweaters, sports equipment or other possessions. Reinstall the closet doors with full-length mirrors, and provide a reflection that appears to double the space.

Like any other major project, redoing a child's room, as previously noted, isn't meant to be an overnight exercise. Finding the right solutions to specific needs takes time. Obviously, it also takes money, although it needn't wipe out your savings if you shop cautiously. Whatever time and money spent on the process should be viewed as a once-in-a-childhood expenditure if you do a good job the first time

Closets with sliding doors enable someone in cramped quarters to store a dresser in space traditionally alloted to hanging storage.

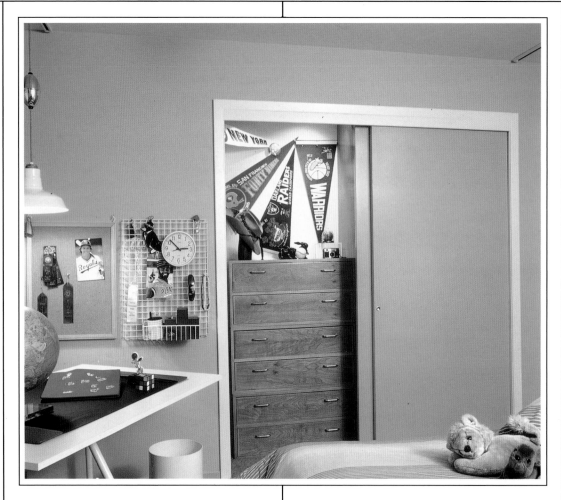

Ironing board hooks assume a new personality as shoe holders in this boy's closet.

around. Smart shopping may take more time, but in the long run it will save effort and money.

CONVERTIBILITY ON A SHOESTRING

Although changing everything in a child's room all at once sounds appealing to achieve a total look, it's probably not feasible for everyone. But even on a shoestring budget there are ways to alter a child's environment inexpensively. First and foremost, there's paint. As mentioned previously, even one simple section of a room recolored can have a monumental effect on a child and some impact from a decorating standpoint. Prudent parents might also take the first step in converting their

A new coat of paint, a change of bedcovers and additional shelving transform what was once a preteen's apple green room (see page 37) into more grown-up space for an 18-year-old.

NO ROOM FOR WHAT'S OUTGROWN

While you attempt to turn your child's dreams into reality, keep in mind a few important points. Although the ultimate goal in this kind of project is creating a setting to handle the immediate needs of its occupant, it is unrealistic to imagine that all features will remain constant. While dolls and other inanimate best friends may be room companions even into adulthood, some things will have to be cast aside. Traditional chairs for small tykes won't support larger folk, nor will closet shelf hideaways support heavier weight than a small child. Don't force your young one to cling to objects outgrown. Just as frustrating as wearing clothes that no longer fit is being challenged to use items that have lost their usefulness or appeal to the child.

One other word of caution: In a child's eyes, a bedroom is a place where things are ever changing. Don't expect the setting you help create to look the same as time passes. From week to week and month to month, the young one who dwells there needs to know his or her needs and interests won't be stifled by a stagnant environment. Support this pattern by filling the room with flexible tools and watch a child strive more for success. But don't condone disorder as a prerequisite of the need for change. Make it easy for a child to find belongings, and the child will store them in an orderly fashion when not in use. Storage holders for specific items promote this as do color-

child's world by acquiring reversible bedcovers. At a moment's notice, they can change the complexion of the place. And because of their proximity to the young sleeper, sheets and bedding make a major impression.

Inexpensive purchases that also pack a lot of punch include colorful bathroom-type throw rugs, bright new desk blotters and vivid fabrics that can add a splash of color to a room by covering bulletin boards or the like.

Those restricted by budget might look to the closet as another place to make an effective low-cost statement. Removing a door to allow space for a makeup center, a puppet theatre or a reading loft costs little time and money. These and many other closet renovations can be done as do-it-yourself projects with limited resources.

Trophies, animal figures and a collection of books promote a sense of self in this teen's room. The contemporary wall system also accommodates a hanging grid for clip-on storage.

coded and labeled containers.

The older a child gets, the more personalized taste becomes. While his or her room should remain practical and functional, it also should reflect a sense of individual style. Fashions and fads have as much a place in a young adult's room as toys do in a nursery. Just as a preschooler takes pride in seeing his or her primitive artistry displayed, a teen promotes a sense of self by showing off movie and rock star posters and other favored objects. These expressions of young adulthood help someone on the brink of maturity establish an identity and create a personal signature.

While striving to provide a setting steeped in convertibility, sound a call for S.O.S. By that I mean look for items that incorporate these three aspects: *simplicity, organization, safety*.

Simplicity implies an object easy enough for a child to handle, whether drawer pull or loft ladder.

Organization translates to an object that helps a child keep his domain well ordered.

And *safety* means an object free of hidden traps that can inflict injury.

DESIGNING FOR THE DISABLED

Nowhere is the need for convertibility and organization in a room more evident than with the disabled. Helping the physically challenged gain better access to their world is no more difficult than designing a space with someone nondisabled. Although this subject will be dealt with at length in the next chapter, for now be mindful that practicality is more important than aesthetics in a project like this. Listen and allow yourself to be innovative to achieve the best results.

ROOM FOR DISCOVERY

What better place for children to discover themselves and the world around them than in their own rooms? Their first and foremost years of exploration begin within its confines. Allowing young ones to choose and color what will surround them is only part of the formula for a successful setting. Just as crucial is the concept of convertibility, providing the kind of flexibility small fry need to master the changes they constantly crave.

Carefully regard the part a parent plays in this scenario. The skill with which you mesh information from your child and input from the marketplace will measure the success or failure of a room to grow. You should be no less careful in nurturing a child's personal environment than you would be in nurturing your own.

CHAPTER 5

Close your eyes and imagine being all grown up in a grade school classroom.

How small and confining the student desks and chairs seem, don't they? How could there ever have been a day when your frame fit into one of them?

As you reflect on that image, realize that's how physically limited children feel every day of their lives as they ask themselves over and over how they will fit into spaces structured for the nonhandicapped.

To those so challenged, there is hope in surmounting such obstacles. At the very least, in their personal surroundings, problems can be resolved through careful strategy and good design. For inspiration, they need only look at a unique young man named Scott. Through a room detailed to his specifications, he showed the world how the quality of life can improve dramatically if an environment caters to personal needs.

A good-natured twelve-year-old, Scott mixed well in the company of strangers, nodding and smiling warmly at them. Judging from faces encountered during a three-week fundraiser while co-designing a space with him, I thought it obvious what kind of first impression Scott made.

Special Spaces for Special Needs

▼▼▼▼▼▼▼▼▼▼▼▼▼▼▼▼▼▼▼▼

"I did that room a long time ago. It's a memory of my past—a very exciting one. It changed my life. It made me have a more positive outlook. It changes your learning toward coping with your disability. I was lucky to meet Tony."

—Scott at eighteen

"It was an excellent idea. It was good for Scott—his first steps on his own. We had to stand back while he talked. And he did it. It was kind of nice."

—Scott's father, Chris

▲▲▲▲▲▲▲▲▲▲▲▲▲▲▲▲▲▲▲▲

Friendly. Mannerly. And typical of an inquisitive boy his age.

No one seemed to notice Scott's sole limitation. Born severely deaf, he could not differentiate sounds. What reached his ears was an audible mix of jangled noises reverberating in a cacophony. His hearing impairment was so severe, he could detect nothing on an audiogram.

Besides youthful determination, what motivated Scott as a child to overcome

personal limitations were sensitive parents, who resolved that his handicap would not hinder his capabilities. Early on in their son's life, they set high expectations for Scott: he would strive to be as knowledgeable and communicative as a hearing person. And he would do that by learning total communication—lip reading, signing and conversational speaking. That way, they reasoned, he would integrate better within the community. Dedicated to developing his intelligence beyond the basics in a standard educational setting, Scott's mother and father insisted on mainstreaming him through regular schools after several years of deaf school education. Obviously, their fortitude paid off since this now college-minded bright young man communicates exceptionally well with hearing people in a clear voice that belies his handicap.

What brought Scott and I together when he was a sixth grader was a sequence of events beginning three years earlier when *Better Homes and Gardens* spotlighted my work in the magazine photo feature "Room to Grow In." Of the dozens of letters readers sent postpublication, nearly half involved children with special needs. Perhaps my background in psychology en-

couraged correspondence from people who felt comfortable writing to someone familiar with such issues. As I responded to each letter, I found myself reflecting on a career that had come full circle, enabling my return to a favored field. Special children, like those in my focus a decade earlier in Pennsylvania, once more tugged at my heart—now for entirely new reasons.

TRANSCENDING HANDICAPS

Working again with the physically limited restrengthened my belief that all young ones share the same basic desires, including a need to personalize their own living quarters. No matter what their mental or physical capabilities, children need a place patterned with them in mind.

So inclined, I seized a public opportunity to create a workable room for a child with limitations. The 1982 San Francisco Decorator Showcase served as my vehicle for this display setting devised with a physically challenged person in mind. A three-room environment tucked away on the top floor of a sprawling three-story home, the site I selected looked out over hilly land bordering a calm bay. Three large multipaned windows let in a steady stream of natural light.

Choosing Scott as the subject of this unique project was hardly happenstance. Realizing how intimidated some people are confronting individuals severely disadvantaged, I intentionally looked for an older child with a somewhat "invisible" disability, namely, deafness. Coincidentally, that very time of year was set aside through presidential proclamation as National Deaf Awareness Month.

Through the Center for the Education of the Infant Deaf, I familiarized myself with many prospective co-designers, all of them under the age of twelve. What drew me to Scott was his impressive ability to speak well despite his condition. Reading lips, he could discern lively conversation by intently watching others, digesting words as they mouthed them.

Working with this bright boy on such an undertaking was a remarkable experience for both of us. While he walked away richer by far in personal pride and self-image, I came away enriched by association with someone so masterful at conquering profound adversity. Before we joined forces, I foolishly saw myself in the role of educator with this young man as my willing student. By project's end, the roles had reversed, much to my surprise and subsequent delight.

SCOTT'S DREAM WORLD

Like any child giving input on a room he will occupy, Scott described in detail what comprised his dream world:
- A home computer area to learn graphic arts skills.
- A stamp collection area to pursue that pastime.
- A hobby spot to build model aircraft.
- A science center to scope land, sky and nearby sea.
- Television space to watch favorite shows.

Scott's adeptness at describing simply the details of his fantasy domain greatly impressed upon me that wordy descriptions aren't always the best. His simple sketches humbled me, too, making me realize the power of plain images. Somehow, this uncomplicated boy, considered "disadvantaged" by virtue of his hearing impairment, was making me see the folly behind the meaning of that term. If one of us were handicapped, more likely it was me for not comprehending sooner some simple truths about Scott's world.

Playing a game with a rainbow of cards, Scott showed me that blue was the color he favored. I marveled at his selection since once again it substantiated my theory about colors corresponding to areas of development. As noted in a previous chapter, blue correlates to eyes, ears and nose, which involve seeing, hearing and smelling. A Master Plan, based on Scott's rudimentary sketches, mirrored that preference. Bright banner blue eventually defined walls and laminate surfaces on natural wood storage units lining one exterior wall.

WHEN YOU WISH . . .

Catering to Scott's wishes was achieved several ways.

Children challenged with physical disabilities share the same dreams as their able-bodied peers. High on this young man's wish list were hobby areas for stamp collecting, television viewing and other pastimes.

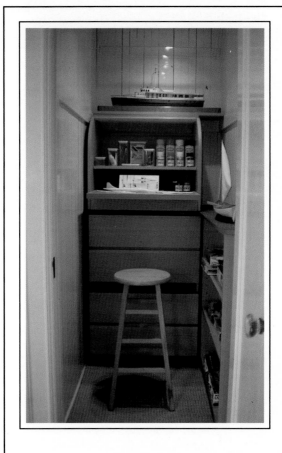

Stripped of clothing rods, this traditional closet converts into an alcove for a model plane enthusiast. Roll top units allow projects to remain "in progress" either in full view or hidden from sight.

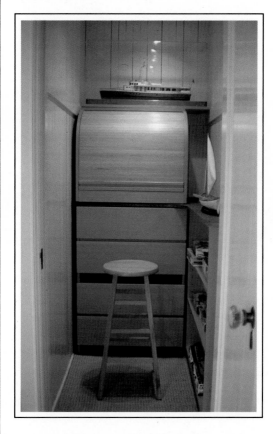

• A pop art stamp poster was hung by one window, reflecting his favorite hobby, stamp collecting.

• A freestanding telescope was placed off to the side, indicating his scientific inclination.

• The handiwork of a model plane enthusiast was evident in the newly configured bedroom closet, devoid of clothing articles, now contained in hall cabinets.

• A boy's burgeoning interest in graphic arts was fueled by the computer firm Atari Corporation, which designed a special program addressing those skills.

• A small TV set, stored inside a rolltop cabinet, fulfilled a preteen's final wish. The perfect place for watching programs was the viewer's trundle bed, doubling as seating space in wide-awake hours.

Lest there be any doubt about who lived here, a mock street sign proclaiming the owner's name was positioned prominently on a wall near the trundle bed. Also testifying to the resident were ample trophies, awards, team photos and athletic gear, including a collection of baseball batting helmets displayed on the wall near the sleep area.

Whimsy lent the final touch to Scott's environment. In the form of jumbo accessories, they detailed the connecting bath decorated crisply in red, white and blue. Taller than the one meant to use this space, the oversized ruler standing near the medicine cabinet could chart Scott's growth, while the oversized toothbrush placed

Easy-to-reach storage and a touch of whimsy define this teen's bathroom.

horizontally above the sink could jokingly remind him of personal hygiene.

SPECIAL TOOLS FOR A SPECIAL CHILD

Besides personalized interest areas and preferential color treatment, what really transformed this setting into Scott's very own were several custom features, including the furniture—all tailor-made to his needs. Styled simplistically from natural wood with versatility in mind, the entire system was modular, consisting of dual drawer base units and rolltop work stations. There also was a bed with a trundle. Designed for easy stacking and rearrangement, the pieces featured colorful accents such as sliding desktop surfaces in bright blue laminate and matching laminate kick panels between the bottom drawer base and the floor. If reconfigured atop one another, the base units would feature a band of blue at each break. For Scott's room, however, each base unit of drawers was topped with either a work station—to serve as an interest area—or a thick cushion, covered in a rainbow-striped fabric that lent the look of a window seat.

"It was a very impressive place," Scott remembers years later of the setting he describes in teen jargon as "hot." In his opinion, "it was so different than all the other rooms in the house that everyone came to look." Obviously, he was unaware that his presence was the main reason the space was always congested with people.

Colorful laminate accents these work stations which roll on casters for total mobility. Blue kick panels between the bottom drawer base and the floor match the writing surface which slides out when the rolltop is open. A simple stool provides sufficient seating.

CUSTOM PLUSES FOR THE DISABLED

For several reasons, Scott's custom furniture system would have been ideal for those wheelchair-bound or severely physically restricted. Four distinct features made it so:

- CASTERS: allowing for total mobility without dismantling the components.
- DRAWER GLIDES: permitting easy use, especially for someone with limited hand strength.
- SLIDE-OUT WRITING SURFACES: enabling the wheelchair-bound to pull a work area over their laps at a height convenient to them.
- STACKABILITY: offering numerous height possibilities as activities require.

DEVICES FOR THE DEAF

What set Scott's room apart besides the aforementioned personal touches were several devices engineered for those with acute hearing loss. The son of a fireman, the twelve-year-old already was familiar with one of them—a telephone unit designed for the deaf and installed at his dad's fire station. Called a Telecommunication Device for the Deaf, the TDD enables the hearing-impaired to relay messages via a display monitor. It works in much the same way a computer display screen shows operator input.

Besides the telephone device, the piece

TELECOMMUNICATION FOR THE DEAF

A TDD is a telecommunication device for the deaf that's available in a portable unit which interfaces with most standard hand-held telephones, including most pay phones. Both the deaf and the speech-impaired benefit from the system, which can be equipped with a paper readout. When someone calls, the telephone receiver is placed in an acoustic coupler on the device, reading sounds made by the caller's TDD as impulses, then printing them on a screen or a paper printout, depending on the features of the particular set.

Using a TDD, a deaf person not only can understand what a call is about, but he or she can respond by typing a message to someone at the other end if that person has a TDD, too. (In some states, the operator will communicate to a caller without a TDD.)

Scott's room not only featured the TDD but auxiliary devices integral to its use, signaling when the phone was ringing. The first device, a tone ringer, concentrated its sound in a frequency range most hearing-impaired can detect. The second device, a gong, was in the base frequency range for customers with severe hearing problems.

An additional accessory essential to TDD users is the master ring indicator, called a signal relay, which activates a light to flash on and off in any lamp plugged into it. (For the deaf/blind, the unit also activates a small electric fan when the phone rings.)

To illustrate the mechanism to those unfamiliar with it, I rigged a buzzer to the lights in Scott's room so showcase visitors could see firsthand a TDD in operation.

Looking more like a typewriter than a Telecommunications Device for the Deaf (TDD), this special tool enables those with hearing loss to relay messages via paper readout and display monitor. It interfaces with most standard headset telephones.

of technology that caused the greatest stir was the Atari computer, introduced at a time when they were just taking hold on the homefront. "People asked me to demonstrate it and show them how to use it," recalls Scott, who was aware that his audience also was "looking for new ideas around the room."

While their son was absorbed in showing off the features in the room he co-designed, the boy's parents delighted in his adeptness at handling such a situation. "It was good for him—his first steps on his own. We had to stand back while he talked. And he did it. It was kind of nice," says his father.

Reflecting on the experience, Scott's mother echoes her husband's thoughts. "It was always positive," she confirms. "It was good exposure for him."

PARENTAL PRIDE

Watching Scott's parents swell with pride as he showed off this equipment and the rest of the setting engineered for him was just part of the pleasure of co-designing this project. Just as thrilling for me was seeing Scott interact with the thousands of strangers who toured the site on a daily basis. As the boy effecting these changes described the room's features and his feelings about them, the public crowded around in awe of this incredible young man. Because he could verbalize and be easily understood, many never even knew he was handicapped. How ironic, I thought, that a deaf child had become the best communicator between those who hear and those who do not. Truly, he was speaking for a silent minority!

Small wonder that after such an experience, Scott's parents saw his social skills improve. This valuable episode in the boy's life had instilled a sense of purpose and a feeling of pride. By "adopting" the environment as his own, even temporarily, Scott had helped create magic for the many who saw it. In the process, he had reshaped his profound handicap into a considerable asset for communicating.

"It changed my life," Scott admits of the experience. "It made me have a more positive outlook," he explains, adding, "it changes your learning toward coping with your disability."

A SPECIAL SPACE FOR YOUR SPECIAL CHILD

Creating a special space for your special child is a challenge worth meeting.

Just as Scott's room encouraged his strengths and strengthened his weaknesses, so, too, can a positive environment for your young one enhance his or her positive skills.

As you help a handicapped child shape a specialized setting, consider the level of frustration that occurs when things are inaccessible.

- Doorknobs or light switches that can't be grasped from a wheelchair.
- Shelves that are too high to reach.
- Cabinets that are too deep to utilize.
- Doorways that prohibit passage.

Working with physically challenged children has convinced me of the setbacks they face when an environment is neither personal nor comfortable. Just as a nonhandicapped child thrives in individualized surroundings, a handicapped child thrives in a space that expresses his or her needs.

In shaping spaces for special children, keep in mind that the end result should provide a good dose of pleasure for the one inspiring it.

CHOICE, COLOR, CONVERTIBILITY

A living and learning space for a child with physical limitations hinges heavily on accessibility. From location of outlets to height of furnishings, the element of choice is crucial here. Consider the ramifications when your child tells you where play and study and sleep areas might best be situated.

Based on the theory that personal color choice corresponds to physical color needs, the handicapped child's palette preference plays a powerful role in a customized room setting. As Scott's blue backdrop indicated, his physical limitations and his social skills improved greatly in an environment colorfully designed by him.

Convertibility also plays a key role in a special room for a special child. As hobbies, habits and interests change, so should

a setting. In support of this, examine the possibility of custom furnishings detailed to your specifications. Convertibility can play a major part in such design, allowing cabinets to be raised or lowered by simple adjustments or desk heights to be easily elevated as the child grows.

No place are height, width or depth measurements more important than in a room for a challenged child. Apparatus such as wheelchairs and other equipment require surroundings that can accommodate their constant presence.

WHAT PRICE CUSTOM DESIGN?

In contemplating custom furnishings, the subject of cost always surfaces. Yet, handicapped design requires no more investment than any other tailor-made merchandise. Knowing that a major amount probably has been spent already on hospital bills and specialized equipment, it's important to view cash outlay for your child's surroundings in perspective. Purchasing furnishings to fit a young one's needs shouldn't be an ongoing process. Devised well and executed properly, good convertible designs should last into adulthood.

One more thought on budgeting money for this kind of expenditure. No matter what you can afford for renovation, paint and all the other particulars are going to cost something. Better to incorporate good designs on a gradual basis, as funds permit, than to do an inferior job posthaste. No one will suffer the consequences of shoddy workmanship more than your child, who doesn't need any more physical challenges.

OTHER SPECIAL PLACES

Designing special places for special people doesn't only mean shaping a personal space for a physically challenged child. It also means providing for young ones, handicapped or not, with a particular interest that requires specialized treatment.

If a child shows extraordinary interest in a certain subject, allow more space for exploring it. Maximize a child's one or two interests if there aren't more that excite him. Don't ever force interests for which a child shows no inclination.

Sometimes, favored childhood pastimes demand more space than ordinarily would be devoted to a hobby. Rather than stifle budding enthusiasm, consider solutions, permitting the topic in question to become the room's focal point. Remember Allison's prospective teenage quarters? From a child who enjoyed growing plants, she matured as a would-be botanist, surrounding herself with all sorts of greenery and an abundance of paraphernalia and publications to help nurture it.

A list of special interests could go on and on, but for our purposes, let's concentrate on four that are among the most popular.

● COMPUTERS: Besides room for hardware equipment, home computer buffs need plenty of space for periphery

Special interests sometimes dictate special needs. Here, a bedroom closet has been converted into open shelving for reptile cases.

equipment, not to mention the software. Dust-free enclosures are important here as well as access to electrical outlets and proper lighting. Be sure to provide enough auxiliary space so a child has room to spread out manuals and paperwork.

● GYMNASTICS: Energetic young bodies who like to exercise should have soft tumble surfaces on which to play. Be careful that no furniture with pointed edges is nearby. A single-sided ladder system secured to the wall saves space while providing an area to stretch and climb. Other gym equipment that might be worth considering: handgrips, dumbbells, barbells, slant boards, and jump ropes. As tempting as it might be to isolate such activity elsewhere in the house, rethink that position. Consider the benefits to a child of having tools of a favored pastime close by when the urge to be active calls.

● NATURE AND SCIENCE: Love of animals and love of plants preoccupy many young ones who marvel at the growth of other life-forms, from gerbils and turtles to flowers and ferns. When nature or science becomes the focal point in a child's room, be sure to provide enough protective surfaces to absorb spills. Proper ventilation and warmth are important, too, especially with respect to animal life.

● MUSIC: Finding room for instruments in a musically inclined child's room may not be easy if the object of their affection is of sizable proportions, like a piano or a set of drums. Where possible, try to set aside space in a child's quarters for his or her special interest if only to encourage it in more secure surroundings. Access to electrical outlets is very important in such a setting as is sound absorption material on the walls. Another consideration in a young musician's room is storage for compositions, music stands and other related items.

A ladder system secured to the wall transforms one corner of this room into an exercise area. Handgrips, slant board, jump rope, barbells and floor mat are among the equipment. With the addition of a single shelf, this unit becomes a work/study area.

JUST HOW SPECIAL ARE THEY?

All children, like all grown-ups, are special, regardless of their physical or mental capabilities. No less worthy is a disabled child who finishes last in the Special Olympics than a nonhandicapped child who accomplishes athletic feats.

Whether superior or slow learner, sighted or blind, all young ones deserve equal treatment and equal chances to succeed in this world.

When viewed as part of the whole human race, these youngest members of society have much in common. They all need love and comfort on a constant basis.

Parents can give their special ones no greater gifts than these.

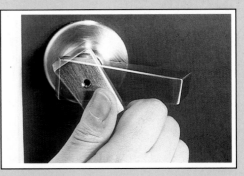

A lever door is one example of Universal Design that can be used by everyone including those with little grip strength or hand dysfunctions.

Adjustable closet rods keep clothes within easy grasp of people who are short or wheelchair-confined.

THE LAND OF UNIVERSAL DESIGN

In a once and future time there is a land where everyone lives unrestricted by structural designs. Young and old. Healthy and infirm. Able-bodied and disabled. Families and mothers-to-be.

No matter what buildings they use, people find them easily accessible. From heavy doors to coin-operated pay phones. From elevators to public bathrooms.

Nowhere does a need exist for special signs showing handicapped access. Nowhere does a problem surface for any segment of society because of physical limitations.

This make-believe land steeped in Universal Design could exist in our tomorrow. Residential and commercial structures could be devised today so that special concessions need never be made for society's less than able-bodied masses.

Designing architecture and merchandise that function for all people is an idea whose time has come. Consider the ramifications if this were done as standard operating procedure.

● Old people impaired by mobility no longer would need to forsake inaccessible homes for institutions.

● Wheelchair-bound people no longer would need to restrict themselves from visiting certain places because of structural limitations.

● Parents toting young ones in strollers no longer would concern themselves with the consequences of being trapped by barriers, like flights of stairs or revolving doors.

As Universal Design authority and architect Ronald Mace of the American Institute of Architects points out in an article appearing in *Designers West* magazine: "Few, if any, people go through life without experiencing disabilities. If we view a person's accessibility needs as they change during his/her life span, it becomes clear that everyone is disabled to some extent at one time or another.

"Many inconveniences we tolerate as young people become true barriers as we grow older, even if we don't become disabled in the technical sense of the word. An infant is helpless or handicapped in a world designed for adults. Loss of hearing, loss of eyesight, arthritis and other symptoms of aging are all disabilities."

Accommodating the needs of people through all phases of their lifetimes starts with awareness of both new technology and usable existing products that address the issue. Most common among the latter are power-operated electric doors and lever-operated mechanisms, such as handles that make opening doors a cinch even for those with restricted hand grasp.

In the wake of modern electronics have come designs profiting those in all walks of life. Controls that beep, illuminate or click to the touch give the user feedback in remarkably easy fashion. So, too, do talking circuits that allow devices like elevator panels and vending machines to provide audio or written messages . . . infrared listening apparatuses that tune in to broadcast programs offering private amplification devoid of extraneous noise . . . remote alarms that sound off if noise- or movement-activated . . . computer systems programmed to do myriad tasks from turning on lights to controlling room temperature.

   The journey to the land of Universal Design is a one-way ticket to an improved world. En route to this exciting destination, experience man's ingenuity for practical ideas that make this planet a better place to live.

Offset water controls (above) make it easy for someone in a wheelchair to turn on the faucet before bathing. A roll-in unit (right) makes showering possible.

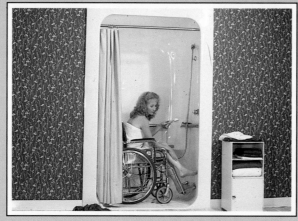

CHAPTER 6

Shared Quarters

Cymbals clashed.

Drums beat.

A lively cadence filled every alcove of the upstairs bedroom, prompting my retreat to a quieter corner of the rambling house.

When the syncopation stopped an hour or so later, the young musician traded places with me in a setting now suitably serene for school study and exercise.

Day in, day out, the routine continued, each of us permitting the other private time in a boyhood room we shared. Sensitive to individual needs for personal space, the two of us worked out this unspoken arrangement as a positive way to address the issue.

The dogged drummer doing rat-a-tat rhythms was my brother, J. R., a spirited soul six years my junior. Our mutual quarters were once occupied by our grandparents and were still filled with some of their Old World possessions. Flowered wallpaper and fine old furniture, fancy rugs and elaborately framed art gave the place a semiformal distinction we respected for what·it represented.

Unless the drawers were opened and the drums displayed, the surroundings belied the fact that two energetic boys lived here. Or so it seemed in my young mind until the first prized memento, a presidential plaque from an inaugural parade, invaded the en-

"The best thing about sharing a room was the personal time with each other. Talking. Playing shadow images on the walls. It was all in the imagination. It's still fresh in my head."

—J. R. Torrice

"It never bothered me when my brother seized the occasion to take over the room and play music. There was an unspoken understanding that personal space could be taken when personal needs were the criteria."

—Tony Torrice

vironment. A tangible symbol of the outside world, it signified that this was now our room. Soon the scene was enlivened with summer camp trophies and athletic awards, lining the valance over the windows. Until then, individual tastes had been submerged under bedspreads and blankets where each set of twin bed sheets told the story of each distinct human being.

The older we grew, the more we stamped our signature into the surroundings, impacting the room with signs of our successes and accomplishments. Science projects and GI Joe dolls . . . super structures of·Lincoln Logs and Legos . . . art posters and treasured carnival prizes . . .

Like many children, I sometimes was

bothered by not having a room of my own. Viewing my sister Margaret's adjacent chamber as a feminine palace complete with a classic canopy bed, I considered her privileged to have someplace all to herself. Yet, my brother and I coexisted compatibly, structuring storage, sleep and other space to our mutual agreement.

Despite restrictions imposed by the room's unalterable decor, we allowed our individual personalities to emerge. The limits set by existing furnishings simply fueled our imagination, yet emphasized that this second-story setting was part of the entire household.

FOUR WALLS, TWO BODIES

Just as a room for a single child should be structured to grow with that child, a room for two children should be shaped to mature with them, reflecting their diverse tastes in the process. Achieving this requires input·from each young one individually so·their respective fantasies about their surroundings may be expressed. Theme rooms which lock a look into place limiting imagination are no more successful for two than for one.

Starting with a Master Plan, sit down

Roman Shades

Window Seat + Storage Area

Loft Bed

Sleep Area

Work Table

Storage Bookcase

Bulletin Board

Study Area

with each child to discover his or her concept of the entire room. Keep in mind as you ask questions, the absent child should be taken into consideration when addressing such issues as sleep and study areas. For example, after asking the one at hand, "Where will you sleep?" then add, "Where will your sister (or brother) sleep?" Always underscore the fact that a final decision will depend on joint approval.

Establishing a sleep area is the most important consideration in a child's bedroom. Once that aspect has been covered, concentrate next on the preferred location of individual work areas. Storage should be the final factor, unless the closet already has been relegated as a sleep or work area. If that's the case, then storage should have a higher priority on your list.

After each child has had a chance individually to visualize the room of his or her dreams, bring them together to share their thoughts and consider compromises. Should their separate Master Plans mesh on major points, deal with those first, reinforcing how good it is they each had the same idea.

On the other hand, if their paper plans disagree, help them negotiate a compromise. Perhaps mutual requests for the same thing can be worked out. For instance, if both want to sleep on the top level of a bunk bed, maybe they both can, by working out an arrangement whereby one gets top billing even months of the year and the other gets it in odd months.

As a parent, your advice in such negotiations is very valuable. Your ability to bring clarity and to exhibit logic in the face of problems should not be taken lightly. The ultimate decision in a conflict of interests should be yours. Take tactful time to offer tangible solutions that allow each person to win and no one to lose.

Keeping both children happy in a room they share is very likely an ongoing effort, but the desire for a congenial environment is no excuse for overindulgence.

Whether trying to please one child or more, parents should never attempt to fulfill every wish young ones express. First determine what dreams are most important, then decide which ones are feasible.

COLORING THEIR WORLD

No matter how many children occupy a space, color remains an essential element. In a shared room, it makes the most sense to localize favored colors in areas closest to the one favoring them.

The bedcovers will say as much about a child to visitors as it will to the child himself. Don't lock yourself into thinking that everything must coordinate in a setting. If more than one taste is involved, try to consider individual desires. Should the mix of patterns your young ones pick tend to distress you, contemplate measures guaranteed to satisfy all sides, including yours. Purchase two reversible comforter covers that match each other on one side and differ on the other, relating to each child's selection. When the room is inhabited, let those living there decide on the motif of the moment. Otherwise, keep the look uniform.

Incorporating colors each child favors in a room both share may mean dividing the color scheme on walls and whatnot. Even one wall covered in each child's chromatic choice will please the ones picking the palette. Other ways to delineate territory belonging to each include colorful blotters, area rugs, throw pillows, curtains and lamp shades. A mere colored light bulb also can individualize part of a child's important personal space.

Because personalities differ, each child's section of the room may look very different from the other. One child may have organized, soft, private space, while another child may have a vibrant, flamboyant setting. Designing a room that addresses both preferences should be the ultimate goal.

Reflecting two tastes in a single space can be successful if color coding is employed. Should Robert like blue and Stephen red, then storage bins and dresser drawers could be done in those respective colors. Continue the association in their bath where washcloths and toothbrushes can carry out the message of what belongs to whom.

A PLACE FOR PRIVACY

Providing for physical needs in a room two children share is only part of the story. It's paramount to address mental needs, too, particularly in the sense of privacy.

Both real and imaginary animal friends enjoy the seclusion of a special closet alcove. In a situation that demands closeness, this may be just the refuge for someone seeking a bit of privacy.

Just because two people, young or old, have to divvy up living conditions doesn't mean that they can't carve out private space for times when solitude is essential. There are several ways to do this, such as the following:

● ROOM DIVIDERS: Standard screens aren't the only way to subdivide space without adding walls. Functional bookcases of the modular, stackable variety act well as partitions, creating nooks and crannies where open space once existed. Besides being able to break up space, they serve well as housing for books, stereos and personal equipment.

● CURTAINS: Just like hospital curtains do in a sickroom for two, simple curtains stretched along a rod can convert open space into sectioned quarters. As sleep or personal needs deem fitting, areas may be cordoned off to eliminate intruding eyes.

● CLOSETS: Whether closets are walkin or otherwise, they can offer seclusion from a situation that cries out with closeness. As mentioned in an earlier chapter, closets can be transformed into meaningful auxiliary space addressing more than storage needs. As an alcove for work or play, they can offer a reprieve from a central area and another person.

● LOFT AREAS: A new level of living can be created in a room with very high

Color-coded and labeled plastic bins help delineate what belongs to whom in a shared room.

ceilings. By taking advantage of vertical space in such a setting, extra room can be eked out of existing space to provide a new sleep or relaxation area.

● ATTICS/BASEMENTS/GARAGE ROOMS/ENCLOSED PORCHES: Because room dimensions may limit possibilities for privacy in certain shared quarters, it's advantageous to look for space elsewhere that can provide this for your children. Periphery places like attics, basements, enclosed porches and rooms over the garage might serve well as settings for spill-over activities. In this way, a confining bedroom need only serve as a sleep time space, while other locations accommodate child's play and child's work.

Stretching living space to accommodate young ones might also be achieved by utilizing a home's interior recesses that otherwise would be ignored. Nooks created by dormers and eves quite possibly can't serve adults. But a small frame only needs small space, and these kinds of cubicles can afford just the right tuckaway spots for real and imagined childhood activity.

Just as my brother and I proved when we were growing up, children sharing a room can work out other arrangements to afford each other privacy. If both parties agree, time could be set aside on a regular basis for each to be in their mutual quarters alone. This could allow time for any personal pleasure—from playing music to spreading out playthings to just enjoying solitude.

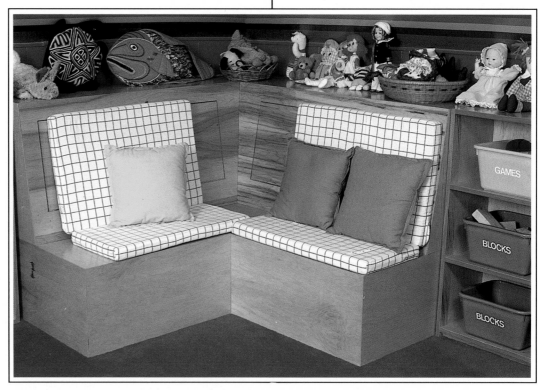

Conquering storage problems in shared quarters often depends on ingenuity as much as space. To make the most of the situation consider furniture like the kind pictured above. Once the cushions are removed, the back of the seat can be opened to reveal hidden playthings (opposite page).

Stuffed play pals find a resting place on this custom unit designed with convertibility in mind. Lid finger holes provide easy access for tiny hands.

One further recommendation about privacy. If children are at an age where side-by-side desk activities seem counterproductive, consider placing their respective work surfaces back to back. Doing this not only eliminates distraction between two people in close proximity, but also provides the feeling of privacy in a shared environment.

STORAGE

Privacy and taste obviously aren't the only issues to be addressed in a room that accommodates two people. The more personal needs to contend with, the more storage to incorporate.

In limited space, organization is essential. In many situations, labeling is an effective means of doing this. Peel-off labels proclaiming the users' names or the container's contents can accomplish this task in creative fashion. Color coding, as mentioned previously, is also a resourceful method for organizing possessions.

Sometimes toys, more than clothes, are the stumbling blocks to adequate storage in children's rooms. There comes a point where satisfying childhood dreams with playthings goes beyond a space's storage capabilities.

In my opinion, the best way to fight overcrowding is a regular six-month routine, eliminating discarded, broken and infrequently used toys. For younger children,

this may be a difficult exercise, but nonetheless necessary. Assigning favored trifles to an "Everyday Toys" box will encourage the child to focus on what's regularly used.

Items less frequently played with should be relegated to a box that's eventually removed from the room. This is another opportunity for parental input. By participating in the weeding out process, you teach children a valuable lesson that extends beyond their toy chest to their wardrobes and other areas that handle personal possessions. Without such guidelines, objects soon take over a room, cluttering a life with too many particulars.

OVERALL CLEANUP

Instilling the need in a child for order and maintenance is a lesson well worth teaching at an early age. Keeping everything clean should be just as important as keeping everything orderly. In a room two share, extra wear and tear probably will mean more time spent on upkeep. Make it easier to do this task by providing cleanup materials close at hand.

Soiled clothing, broken toys and a preponderance of "stuff" can be avoided if some good habits are encouraged early on.

FURNITURE

Finding furniture that conforms to a single space two children are sharing requires

just as much attention as outfitting a place for someone solo.

Convertibility works its magic for two as well as for one. If properly chosen with convertibility in mind, furnishings for joint tenants of a childhood room will endure for years, meeting both occupants' needs until one moves on. Even then, the one remaining should find the old furnishings still fit well into the new picture.

Bunk beds obviously maximize room in confined quarters, but they aren't the only way to solve the matter of two sleepers in a single sleeper's space. Trundle beds concealing one unit work well, as do new-fashioned Murphy beds that enable a sleeping surface to be tucked away. Still other effective means for dealing with this issue are sleeper sofas and Japanese-style futons. Both fold up easily when not in use.

If children are at an age where a double bed or larger will suit their joint needs, this might be an alternative. Before investing in a solitary unit, however, keep in mind the two personalities who will be sharing it. If sibling rivalry is an ongoing battle, confining those fighting to the same sleeping unit won't help win the war!

Rooms with enough wall height for a loft afford another way to create a separate sleep area without swallowing up central floor space.

What to avoid in furnishing a child's room is just as important as what to take advantage of. Something that may not be the best solution is a waterbed, which not only consumes major immovable space but also causes problems if children are care-

Once a catchall, this renovated attic space now accommodates many children in group play. Sleep, study and storage all blend resourcefully.

During the day, this room's young occupants amuse themselves by drawing on a large chalkboard. During naptime and nighttime, the board drops down to reveal the traditional bed pictured on the opposite page.

less. Consider the consequences of a room overflowing with liquid because a stray pair of scissors sliced into a waterbed's polyurethane pouch. Waterbeds can also create a serious problem for children who tend to view their sleeping surface as a part-time trampoline. One advantage of waterbeds, however, is the comfort and support they supply to bed-confined children. Since each situation is different, be sure to weigh the pros and cons of such bedding.

THE BIG SQUEEZE

Because of the measurements of standard size furnishings, it's good to know the least amount of space two people can share. A room measuring eleven by fourteen feet approximately is the minimal living requirement for a couple of roommates. Realize that there are some spaces that physically can't handle all the needs of two humans, even little ones. If that's the case, forgo cramming everything both occupants own into such tight quarters. Limit small surroundings to sleep, and reevaluate other locations in the home for childhood play and learning areas.

Card tables and collapsible TV trays are worthy acquisitions for those suffering space crunch. By providing work and play surfaces that store easily, auxiliary trays and tables provide temporary relief from an inadequate room setting.

SPECIAL SITUATIONS

As with anything in life, special situations often require special treatment. That's the case if the two sharing space in a home have circumstances that dictate a different set of rules.

If the age gap between joint tenants is wide, severe logistical problems can occur unless certain steps are taken. A teen rooming with a toddler, for instance, may spell trouble if the tastes of one overtake those of the other. It's important that each person's interests be reflected, instilling positive feelings in emerging personalities.

A preteen may want to start collecting posters and other paraphernalia, while a younger sibling may prefer familiar toys and other childhood trappings. Offer that budding adult a private place like a bulletin board or a single wall or even the back of a door to house memorabilia. On the other hand, do not forget that a younger child needs a place for juvenile interests such as stuffed animals and dolls.

Another situation that entails special consideration is a space shared by a physically challenged child and a nonhandicapped sibling. In such cases, keep in mind that accessibility is a prime factor in creating a place where both can be properly accommodated.

SEPARATE IDENTITIES

Just because two young people share the same space doesn't mean they share the same needs and desires. Even twins need to emerge as separate entities rather than carbon copies of each other.

Each child ultimately wants to know that his or her personal imprint is taking hold in a room, be it on the bed where a special stuffed toy is propped or on the wall where a budding attempt at artistry is displayed.

In a young child's mind, each visual image creates impact. Therefore, the differences in a room two share make all the difference in the world. The parental eye may view mutual quarters their offspring share as a hodgepodge of possessions and a

Strong hooks keep a convertible custom bed safely latched away when it's meant to stay in an upright position.

crazy quilt of tastes and interests. But in their children's eyes, this space that caters to both personalities is what makes it work on a daily basis.

Coexisting in a room with a brother or sister is rarely ever an easy experience day in and day out. But on the other hand, the bonding that may occur from sharing common ground can endure a lifetime and inspire everlasting role models. Allow both children to personalize part of their everyday world and foster self-image and mutual respect, which will help them now and throughout their lives.

Catering to individual needs and tastes in shared quarters may start by simply allowing each child to choose his or her own bed linens.

PART TWO

Living and Learning

The Nuts and Bolts of Building Rooms

Allowing children to have an impact on their personal environment is as important to development as early education.

Yet, all too often parents stifle their son's and daughter's *signatures* in a room. They do this either by imposing their own childhood fantasies or by enforcing a "nothing goes" policy in a nondescript setting. Equally stifling for altogether different reasons are parent-sanctioned rooms steeped in childish "stuff" bombarding the senses from every angle.

What this book demonstrates is the wisdom of rethinking those philosophies by underscoring the value of children's rooms that reflect children's tastes. Since they spend more time in their own rooms than anyone else, children should be the primary judges of how these surroundings look and suit their needs. In no better way can they explore on a daily basis who they are, what they are and where they are. This assures establishing self-confidence and positive self-image along the way.

As parents recognizing the significance of this exercise, you must realize the important part you play. While a young mind deserves a chance to express ideas, one cannot expect someone at a tender age to understand the ramifications of every no-

A Place for Living

"To make sense to the child, information, instructions and demands for obedience must correspond to the child's available touch, smell, sight and muscular movement."

**—Joseph Chilton Pearce,
Magical Child**

tion. Cost, construction and other specifications are adult concerns, emphasizing the need for parental guidance in carrying out Master Plans that junior members of the household devise.

To simplify the process of enacting these plans, this chapter serves as a quick reference guide. It pinpoints furnishing options by category, listing ways to achieve different looks on different budgets. In so doing, it addresses both ready-made and custom designs.

Before deciding on any kind of furniture, be sure to measure accurately the room's

periphery, including the height from the floor to the window sills and the depths of the closets. Make a drawing of the room, noting exactly where the outlets, heaters and vents are located. By doing this, you eliminate the frustration of purchasing furnishings that do not fit the space for which they were intended. To make the selection process easier, take measurements and any fabric or carpet swatches with you when you shop.

As you embark on this journey to your child's dream-come-true room, try to put yourself in your child's shoes. From his or her level, look around the environment, noticing what's out of sight and out of reach from that vantage point. Make note of that so you can remedy the situation if need be. Now, it's time to begin a shopping expedition in the company of that resident expert—the boy or girl initiating those changes in your home.

A PLACE TO SLEEP

Placement of a child's bed is the most important aspect in his or her room. As much as possible, allow the child to dictate where the sleeping surface should be, paying close attention that the space chosen doesn't interfere with the swing of a door, the location of an air or heat vent, or any other obstruction. Being near a window or the corner of a room may hold special meaning, however, so try to offer a similar option if the child's first choice isn't feasible. Special consideration should be made for a handicapped child who may have fewer bed placement options, depending on specific needs.

Ideally, a sleep area should afford room on either side of the bed for a small nightstand. It can serve as a handy surface for all kinds of necessities, from bedtime storybooks to a box of tissues to a late night glass of water. If a room's measurements won't allow such treatment, consider keeping a rolling cart nearby like the kind artists use. Fill its storage compartments with all the items a young sleeper considers essential.

To determine the style of bed to purchase for your child, let space, cost and convertibility be your guide. In tight quarters, a canopy might tend to overwhelm the site, particularly if the ceilings are low. Conversely, in large quarters, a single bed may look lost. Measure the room's dimensions, including the ceiling height, so you won't be unpleasantly surprised when an oversized or undersized purchase arrives.

Before making any decisions, realize how multifunctional a bed can be. There's no need to view this most essential element in a child's room solely as a piece of furniture for sleep. Depending on the model selected, a bed can perform double duty as a soft play surface, a reader's retreat, a study station, a storage unit or an extra

sleep area for an overnight guest (in the case of a bunk or a trundle).

The best kind of construction material for children's furnishings is strictly a matter of taste. While wood gives a traditional, warm look with natural beauty that lasts for years, colorful metal and plastic bring a joyful element to a youthful setting.

With all that in mind, examine the op-

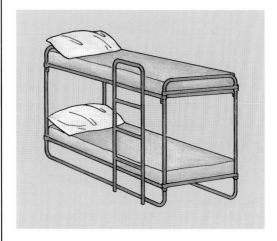

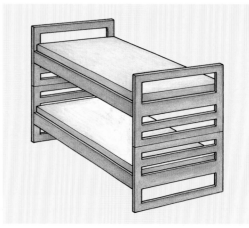

Bunks supply extra sleeping without consuming extra floor space.

tions in the marketplace, some of which are listed below in alphabetical order.

● BUNK BEDS: A popular choice for spaces accommodating dual sleepers, bunks provide extra sleeping while not swallowing additional floor space. Linked one above the other with a ladder that makes the top accessible, they usually are designed so they can also be used

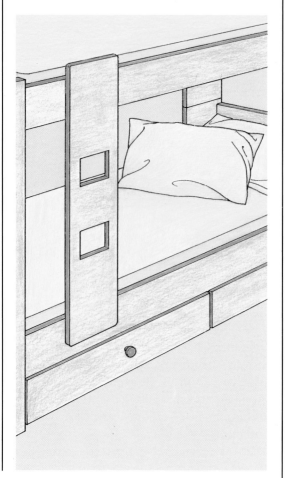

as separate units. Be sure that the upper bunk is not only far enough away from the ceiling to prevent a sleeper from hitting his head, but also far enough away from the lower unit to give adequate head room to the sleeper below. Also be mindful of securing the unit to a wall so it won't topple over with weight on it. And be sure that the child is old enough to sleep in the upper bunk without falling out. As an extra precaution, provide a soft floor surface adjacent to the bed in case falls occur.

One other consideration: Because of the vertical space they use, bunk beds visually tend to overpower some rooms.

• CANOPY BED: Sleeping surfaces with regal appeal, canopy beds feature an overhead framework with a rooflike covering often frilly or see-through. Appealing to children because of the sheltered feeling they provide, canopies may be quite costly because of their construction. Although many can be assembled on location, some cannot, so it's important to know the dimensions of your child's doorway before you invest in one. Keep in mind that the height of this unit may restrict its use in some rooms.

Two other considerations: If cost prohibits such a purchase, you may achieve a similar effect with a simple piece of fabric suspended over a standard bed. Another option along the same lines is a bed tent, which offers the sleeper a camplike environment.

• CAPTAIN'S BED: Like the built-in

Regal-looking canopies may appeal to some children who like the sheltered feeling they provide.

beds used by ship captains, the ready-made units named after them feature a base comprised of multisize drawers. Usually much higher than a standard bed, the captain's version often has a raised ridge circumventing the mattress.

● FUTON: A Japanese-style portable sleeping surface, a futon is a thin, fabric-covered, lightweight foam mattress that folds in half or in thirds. Easily stored, it offers an ideal solution for an overnight guest. Its cost is generally reasonable.

One other consideration: Although usually made of firm foam, a futon may not be the best everyday sleep surface from the standpoint of support.

● LOFT BED: Rooms with very high ceilings, or doorless closets reinforced with a high sturdy shelf, provide the possibility of a built-in loft. An ideal retreat for a young napper, a loft allows an on-

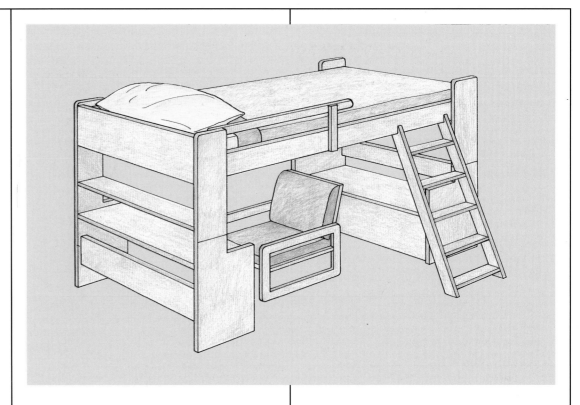

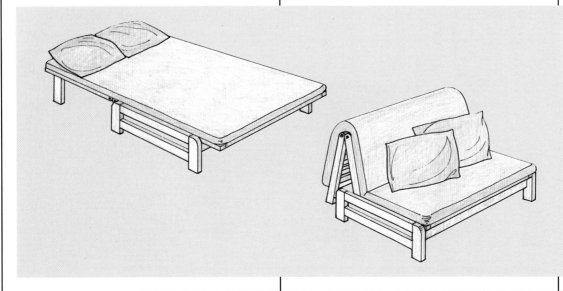

Aside from acting as a sleep surface, the bed can also serve as an appropriate spot for study and play. One unit that works well, especially in limited spaces with high ceilings, is a loft bed like that pictured above. Another space-saving sleep option is the futon (left) which folds in half or in thirds thereby serving as adequate seating or allowing for easy storage.

high vantage point that appeals to the pint-size set who usually need to look up to most of the world. A ready-made version is available as a freestanding unit with a sleep space on the top and varied study and storage configurations on the bottom.

Two other considerations: As with bunks, it's wise to secure freestanding units at least to a single wall. Because they afford the chance for a serious fall, lofts should be built with secure, sturdy ladders and adequate side rails.

● MURPHY BED: Named after the man who invented it at the turn of the century, the Murphy bed swings up or folds into a closet or cabinet when not in use. A good space-saving option, it provides instant accommodation for an overnight guest.

One other consideration: This bed may require adult assistance in lowering or lifting and should not be left to a small child to open or fold away.

● PLATFORM BED: A style of bed that's built on a raised box, it offers possible storage in the form of pull-out drawers.

● SLEEPING BAG: A lined, zippered bag originally made for outdoor use, a sleeping bag is ideal for accommodating a young sleep-over guest. It should not be considered an option for a permanent sleep surface since it does not provide the kind of support growing bodies require.

● STANDARD BED: The most versatile sleep surface on the market, the standard

Constructed so that it can fold or swing into a closet or special cabinet, the Murphy bed may be a good way to accommodate a child's overnight friends.

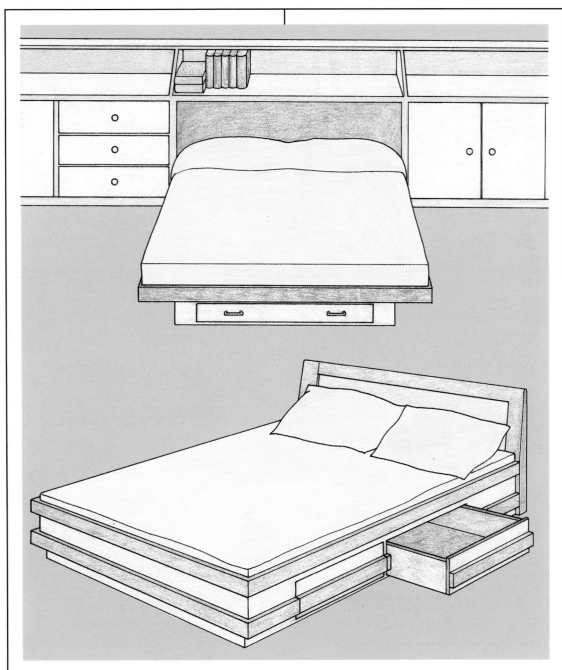

Built on raised boxes, platform beds offer storage in the form of pull-out drawers.

bed on a metal Hollywood frame usually is the most reasonable. Available in four sizes from single to king, it also is the most readily available.

● TRUNDLE BED: A two-in-one sleep unit, the trundle contains an additional bed that either pulls out like a drawer from the front or the side, or collapses on a metal frame that rolls under the top unit when not in use. The drawer model provides the possibility of serving as simple storage.

One other consideration: If casters are a feature, be sure your floor surface does not impede their rolling motion.

● WATERBED: A water-filled mattress bag, a waterbed may not be the best solution for a young sleeper. Not only is it immovable, it causes problems if children are careless with sharp objects that can puncture the pouch containing liquid. Similar problems could be incurred with air mattresses. On the other hand, bedridden children may benefit from such sleeping surfaces, which contour comfortably to their body and may alleviate bedsores.

● YOUTH FANTASY BED: Custom beds that resemble racing cars, space ships or other forms may be novel, but they tend to time-lock a room. A child's changing tastes may not warrant this kind of expense. If a child has problems with bed-wetting, you might want to forgo a fancy mattress until toilet training has been accomplished. Foam or a rubber pad could be a better alternative in this situation.

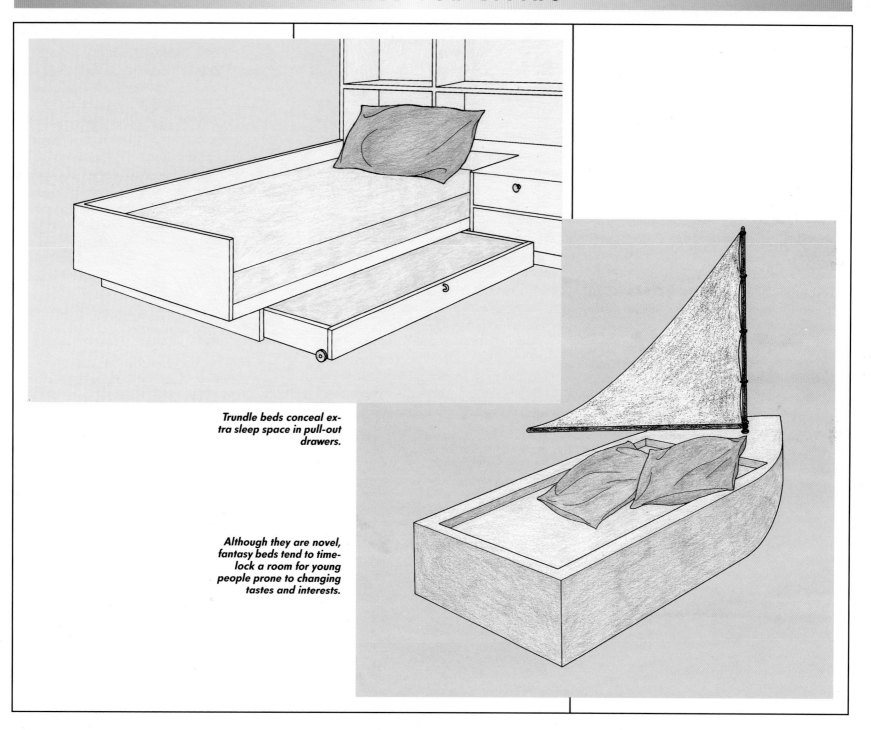

Trundle beds conceal extra sleep space in pull-out drawers.

Although they are novel, fantasy beds tend to time-lock a room for young people prone to changing tastes and interests.

A QUESTION OF SAFETY

Although bunk beds and other dual units often entice leaping limbs, be careful that your children don't equate their sleep surfaces with trampolines. Not only is there danger involved with such activity, but this kind of treatment shortens the life span of any sleeping unit.

As parents, you should instill an understanding about safety. Small children, especially those making the transition from a crib to a bed, need to realize there are limits to what conventional sleeping surfaces allow. Providing bed rails and sleep guards as safety measures makes good sense, as does placing a bed in a room's corner thereby securing two sides.

Care also needs to be taken if a young child's bed is placed by a window. A unit that's high off the ground may enable an energetic climber to crawl up and out of an opening. Latches preventing windows from opening all the way, and window rails are two devices for preventing such accidents from happening.

Bedroom safety also brings up the subject of dangers such as fire and other disasters. It's always a good idea to plan a couple of family escape routes in case something serious occurs. In the event of an emergency, you might ensure your child's well-being by supplying a rope ladder near a window. Put a label on it that's visible from the outside so that rescuers will know which room is occupied by your little one.

BEDDING

Mattress support is as important as the kind of bed you choose. Because a young sleeper has a light frame, don't make the mistake of purchasing inferior products. Not only is it important for growing bodies to have good support, it's smart to buy with an eye toward the future. As a child gets older and heavier, he or she may still be able to sleep comfortably on the same childhood bed. To distribute wear evenly, be sure to rotate the mattress on a regular basis (every six months or so).

Long-term investments demand careful attention to guarantees and warranties.

Choosing soft bedding over firm is a matter of personal preference. Let the person meant to sleep on that surface decide what feels best. Allow your child to sit down and lie down on several models before a decision is made. At the same time, child-test the pillows, checking for comfort of firm versus feather. Be careful to consider allergies and washability before a final decision is made.

BED LINENS

Soft, comfortable covers that brush against a young face add greatly to a good night's sleep. A warm blanket, a quilted bedcover and a soft pillow envelop a child in a dreamy cocoon. Small wonder that the covers one sleeps under are just as important as the surface slept on.

Except for a floor covering that's made of fibers, there's no better place than a bed for a child to experience physical contact with texture. Soft or coarse, colorful or plain, cold or warm, fabrics play a vital role in the development of tactile senses. Pillows serve as cozy comfort for a child deep in sleep. Joined by a favorite stuffed play pal, the picture is complete.

Unlike the rest of the room, the bed is one place where theme characters may prevail, enlivening the sheets that surround a young body. In a shared room, be sure to let each individual pick his or her bed linens.

CUSTOM COVERS

If your budget allows for custom-designed fabrics, consider bedcovers that are reversible. They stretch your money by offering an additional option and supplying a longer-lasting item that guarantees convertibility as a child grows. Pillow cases can show an alter ego if they're sewn with two different materials inside and out. So, too, can comforters that are covered in reversible fabrics of varying colors. In a room where two dwell, dual-sided comforters have the added advantage of providing a uniform look when that's desirable. Otherwise, their flip sides reflect separate tastes. Comforter cases, called duvet covers, are readily available in department stores.

Custom fabric allows for coordination of window coverings, canopies and other features in a child's room. But be sure to exercise restraint, not only because of the

CUSTOM VS. READY MADE

The road to furnishing a child's room is a two-way street. In one direction lies ready-made furniture, available through department stores and other outlets. Along the opposite route lies custom-designed furniture, crafted to individual specifications. Besides cost, there are other reasons to consider—or to forgo—each as an option.

WHY CUSTOM-MADE?

- Means anything goes from finishes to styles to colors.
- Allows for built-in convertibility features.
- Enables design that fits space exactly.
- Offers opportunity for better materials providing more value for money spent.
- Affords more variety in both wood and laminate finishes than available commercially.
- Permits handicap design features zeroing in on special needs.
- Provides possibility of adding coordinating pieces even years later.

CUSTOM-MADE DRAWBACKS

- Demands usually a bigger cash outlay than ready-made.
- Restricts buyer with immovable built-ins.
- Affords no opportunity in most instances for changing your mind and returning merchandise.
- Demands longer wait for merchandise in some cases because of construction.

cost involved, but also because overdoing the effect will create a theme room that is easily tired of. If there's any doubt in your mind about where fabric should go, ask your young one to share his or her preferences.

Whether custom or ready-made, fabrics in a child's room should always be washable. Fine quality goods like silk and expensive linen don't belong in a setting where small sticky fingers can do permanent damage. Besides the usual materials, consider the same kind of heavy nylon fabric used to make tents and ski parkas. Often available quilted with cotton batting in reversible colors, it is an ideal bedcovering that's warm and washable.

If a child's bed is a trundle or another style that functions as more than a sleep surface, consider having fitted covers custom-made with contour corners. This fitted boxed look adapts well to daytime play especially with the addition of bolster pillows, serving as sturdy back cushions for children absorbed in nonsleep activity.

When weighing the cost of ready-made versus custom fabric in a child's room, think about the benefits of a long-term investment with built-in convertibility features.

STORAGE

S.O.S.
Simple. Organized. Safe.
Those are the bywords of good storage in a child's room.

WHY READY-MADE?

- Offers availability in all price ranges.
- Affords possibility of immediate acquisition if stocked.
- Permits prepurchase examination unless special-ordered.
- Provides easy shopping opportunities at many department stores and specialty shops.
- Allows buyer in some instances to return merchandise for exchange.
- Supplies opportunity for mail-order purchases through nationally distributed catalogs.

READY-MADE DRAWBACKS

- Limits number of choices, colors, styles and finishes that may be purchased.
- Requires matching pieces be purchased before style discontinued or stock depleted.
- Provides less durability if poorer construction materials used.
- Limits buyer: What you see is what you get.

ALWAYS BE PREPARED

Regardless of whether you choose ready-made or custom furniture for a young one, be prepared when you go shopping. Besides bringing paint and fabric samples along, take a copy of the Master Plan, listing all measurements.

Some final advice: Compare prices before you make a selection. Don't let cost be the only determining factor, however. Check a store's delivery and return policies carefully to save yourself unwelcome surprises later. Also be aware of any added costs and/or penalties that may be incurred if you special-order a piece in a custom finish or fabric. Usually you pay dearly for the privilege of doing so with either no possibility of rejecting the merchandise once it arrives, or the likelihood of paying a penalty for changing your mind.

Before putting anything away, think about the person who will be retrieving it on a regular basis. Find an obvious place for belongings—shoes on a shoe rack, socks in a drawer. Then ask yourself a couple of questions: Will tiny hands be able to grasp the knobs and open the drawers easily? Will a short frame be able to reach certain shelves without climbing?

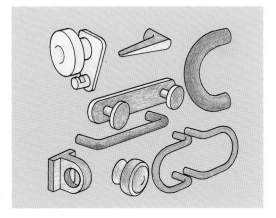

Small hands have trouble grasping certain hardware. Let them test store displays to determine their capabilities.

Keeping storage simple means keeping it accessible, too. Children who find access to their possessions burdensome will act out their frustrations, keeping things in disarray. As noted previously, small fingers lack sufficient strength and motor skill to pull very large or very small knobs. Better choices in children's furnishings include units with either drawer pulls that little hands can grasp, or drawers with glides that young ones can slide open and closed, often by tugging lightly on a finger grip or groove.

Another simple alternative for children is a drawer or cabinet design with touch latches that release the opening mechanism when slight pressure is applied. Also easy for children to grasp are drawer units with small finger-hole openings.

Children who face special physical challenges may require special consideration in storage suitable for them. Door handles of the lever variety are more accessible to the wheelchair confined than standard doorknobs.

In all instances, let the one who will be using these designs on a daily basis determine what hardware is the easiest to handle. Perhaps the best way to prevent potential barrier problems is by allowing a child to test hardware store displays before furniture is purchased.

Hand in hand with simplicity is organization. Keeping a room orderly goes beyond having the furniture neatly arranged. Whether toys, clothes or assorted sundries, personal possessions should be stored in an orderly fashion in locations decided upon by the owners themselves. Let proximity to task areas serve as a guide. A computer work station, for instance, needs storage nearby for hardware, software, paper and assorted manuals.

To help young ones accomplish the goal of adequate, accessible storage, consider color coding or labeling drawers or other containers. Especially effective in a room more than one share, these methods of organization add an element of personalization to a youthful environment.

Color-coded storage has the distinct ad-vantage of being able to coordinate with a room's color scheme from fabrics to walls to floor covering. For some handicapped children, this marking method is particularly beneficial, enabling them to identify their worldly goods very easily. In such a situation, blue might delineate toys, green might distinguish games and red might signal school supplies. Let your child choose the colors.

A child's color preference need not be restricted to open areas. Sometimes, the inside of storage can contain a colorful accent. Fabric or decorative paper used as lining makes a personal statement while keeping drawers clean, too.

Labeling storage with familiar words has the added bonus of helping young ones learn language. Blocks. Marbles. Stickers. Pencils. These and other objects constantly used by little ones can be placed in containers appropriately labeled with marking crayons or peel-off vinyl letters. To further promote language skills, labels might mark room accessories such as the clock, the chair, the desk, etc. As terms are mastered, labels can be removed and additional items singled out for marking.

BUYING A DRESSER

Because a child's dresser will be pressed into duty on a daily basis, consider more than decorative appeal when buying one. Study construction carefully. Drawers should be sturdy enough to hold weight yet pull out easily when a child tugs on the handles.

Just as important as dresser construction is height. The young one whose belongings are being stored should be able to reach them without straining. Inaccessibility is frustrating for anyone at any age let alone a child trying to master his surroundings.

Although the dresser for a child should be scaled to a child's size, it should not be so small that it lacks adequate storage. Ideally, there should be enough drawers to accommodate essential clothing items.

If limited floor space makes storing a dresser a problem, consider placing the piece inside either a walk-in closet or a standard closet with sliding doors. One side can be devoted to hanging clothes, while the other can be relegated to furniture suitable for storing wardrobe foldables and other possessions.

As you contemplate the right dresser to fulfill your child's needs, consider convertibility factors. Modular units with stacking features give a child room to grow.

ALTERNATIVE STORAGE

Freestanding units like dressers and nightstands may be the most common form of bedroom storage, but they needn't be the first and last resort.

Sleeping units with built-in drawers under the bed frame work well as clothing and toy storage. So do window seats, stackable plastic milk carton carriers and wire baskets. The latter may need liners, however, to prevent small objects from falling through openings.

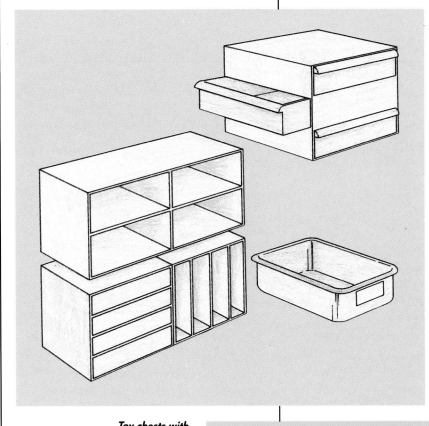

Storage that stacks offers varied looks and room to grow.

Toy chests with safety latches are by far the wisest.

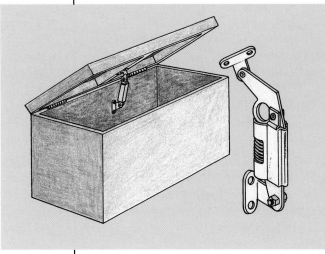

Sturdy cardboard or plastic storage boxes, like the kind sold in a variety of colors, are another affordable storage alternative. Tuck them away neatly labeled under a bed and little ones can reach their belongings easily.

SAFETY FIRST

Safety should always be a prime consideration in a child's room. Examine everything with a keen eye, checking to see if small fingers could get caught easily in drawers, or if storage piled on high could easily tumble onto small unsuspecting bodies. Perhaps drawer stops are all that's needed to deter some accidents.

Don't assume the furniture is foolproof just because it's sold commercially. Check to be sure nails aren't exposed, wood isn't splintered, or paint isn't toxic. Stackable units, like modular cubes, should be given the once-over to be sure they're secure, if not to each other then to the wall they're placed against.

Scrutinize bookcases and shelves, too, ascertaining if anything too heavy has been placed on them that would make them prone to tipping over. If the shelves are glass, be certain there are no jagged or sharp edges. In rooms for the very young, glass is not a good idea.

Toy chests also deserve some attention on a safety check. Make certain that lids aren't so heavy they could easily fall, hurting someone looking for a favorite plaything. Seek out chests equipped with safety latches.

THE CLOSET

One of the most overlooked territories in a child's kingdom is the bedroom closet. A space that can assume magical qualities, it doesn't need to be relegated strictly for storage.

Because their wardrobes don't consume much vertical hanging space, the very young can have their clothing placed at lower vantage points in the closet, thereby relieving major space for other uses.

Devoid of its door, the traditional closet can serve as an open area sectioned into special quarters like a napper's loft or a student's alcove. The doorway opening might also be transformed into a puppet theater with the addition of a piece of fabric slit with openings large enough to accommodate a cloth cast of characters.

Although older children require more space for their larger clothes, they may also be able to create special niches in their closets for favorite pursuits. Computers and other technical equipment might fit well into such an alcove. So, too, may a makeup center.

Electric outlets and good lighting are two features to consider seriously if a closet is being transformed into a unique haven.

Backs of doors also have storage possibilities. Their large flat surfaces are ideal for housing clipboards, bulletin boards or standard shoe pouches, serving well as catchalls for childish treasures.

STORING TINY TREASURES

Providing adequate storage in a child's room means more than thinking big in terms of containers. It also means thinking small. The trappings of youth are often assorted wee treasures that can create disorder if they aren't properly arranged.

There are many inexpensive ways to corral tiny treasures. Empty unused paint cans with no sharp edges provide handy storage for marbles, craft supplies, baseball cards and other items. To add a special touch, label and spray paint the exterior if the one using the containers sees fit to do so. Once again, let the child choose the color.

Other versatile storage ideas that are low cost include the following:
- Molded plastic bowls.
- Hanging wire produce baskets of the tiered variety used in kitchens.
- Wall-hung grid systems with hooks that accommodate anything from clocks to calendars, and shelves that do likewise.
- Clean take-out Chinese food containers.
- Empty plastic milk cartons.
- Cardboard storage files.
- Recycled ice cream containers.

Many parents mistakenly equate the need for order with the judgment to keep everything that isn't essential hidden behind doors. While tidiness is an admirable trait, it's important to allow some of a child's treasures to be within view. Seeing

favorite objects that rekindle memories of summer vacations or school friends reassures a child of the personal relationship each has to the world around him. These may include family photographs and school pictures.

If illuminated by a night-light, these visible belongings provide extra security for a sleeper fearful of the dark.

A PLACE TO STUDY

Quiet space, adequate work surface, comfortable seating, good lighting and close access to storage are all criteria for an adequate study area. A laboratory for discovery away from school, it can create a climate for fermenting ideas or frustrating the learning process entirely, depending on how well you supply the necessary tools.

A standard desk not only provides sufficient work surface and storage but easy access to drawers. Although the next chapter will focus on specific learning centers, some overall ideas on the subject may be helpful at this point.

If your child is particularly hard on the furniture he or she uses, your first consideration in a desk may be one with a protective surface impervious to ink and liquid. To childproof other kinds of desks, add a colorful blotter or a clear piece of plastic cut to fit the top.

A blotter with a splash of color that matches other room accessories can also serve in a small way to unify a room's look. A more elaborate way of achieving the same result is acquiring a desk that's part o. a suite of coordinated furnishings.

Besides construction, the most important aspect of a desk is its design. No matter what style you choose, it should have a large enough surface to handle the average workload. If your child has a special hobby or other reason for spreading out projects, it might be wise to select a model with a larger-than-average work surface.

Although standard desks suit most needs, there are several other options in the marketplace that may be worth considering. Listed in alphabetical order are some of them.

● ART/DRAFTING TABLE: A work surface designed to be slanted to accommodate art-in-progress, an art or drafting table lends itself well to other projects that require surfaces larger than a standard desk. Lack of storage may make this unit undesirable as a sole place of study. Some models may also lack an adequate ledge for securing writing implements.

● COMPUTER DESK: Designed to house a home computer system, such a desk normally comes equipped with shelves specifically geared for periphery equipment. Because of the electrical needs for operating computer systems, myriad outlets are fairly standard features. Before investing in one, make sure there's enough room for related supplies like manuals, as well as an auxiliary work surface.

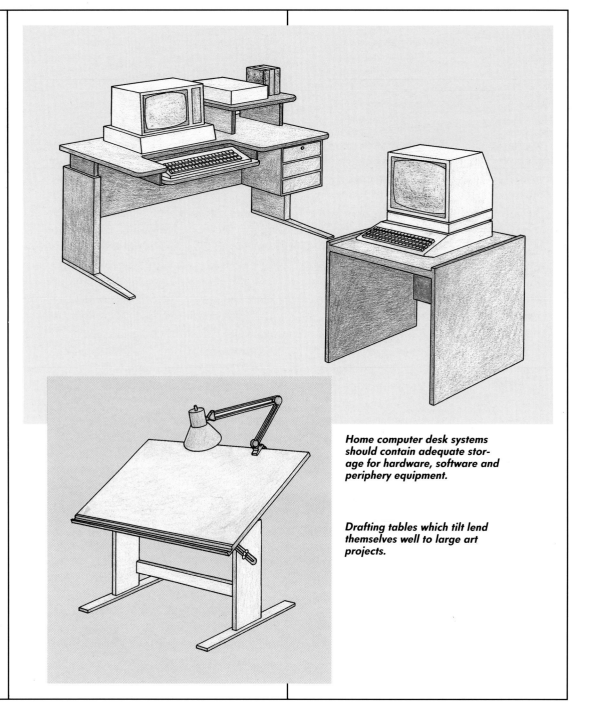

Home computer desk systems should contain adequate storage for hardware, software and periphery equipment.

Drafting tables which tilt lend themselves well to large art projects.

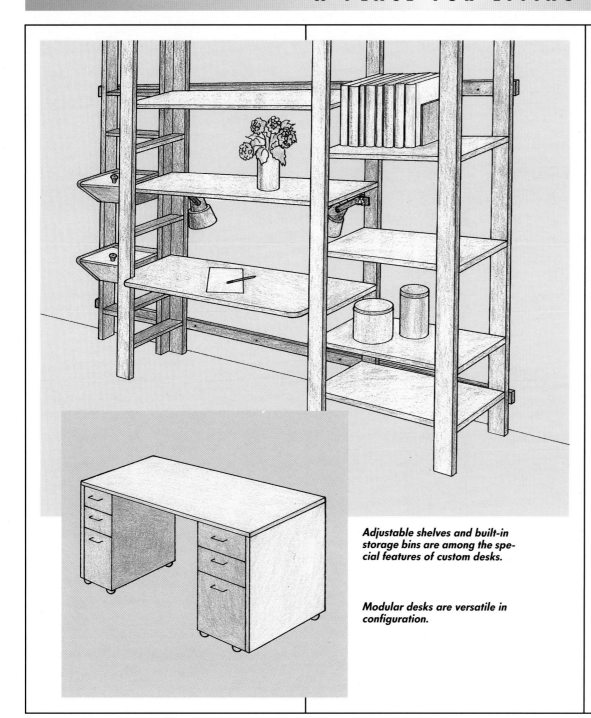

Adjustable shelves and built-in storage bins are among the special features of custom desks.

Modular desks are versatile in configuration.

Two other considerations: Although ideal for the purpose they serve, computer desks may not be the best answer for multipurpose work stations because of their limited surface for other tasks. Since shelves that accommodate hardware and software are often placed high on the front of the unit above the monitor, vision is restricted and, consequently, so is natural light from the front. Furthermore, overhead shelf heights may be out of reach to some children.

• CUSTOM DESK: Generally an expensive investment, a custom study desk affords the opportunity for special features such as swivel surfaces, turntables and other elaborate details. Well worth the cost for a child with special physical needs, custom units should be well thought out before any construction begins.

One other consideration: A custom desk designed with a ladder system, like the kind employed in Michael's room in Chapter 2, provides the possibility of climbing the side so a child may have easy access to higher shelves and storage.

• MODULAR SYSTEMS: Modular units such as stackable cubes provide two interesting options. First, they afford multiple configurations of assorted drawers, bins and cabinets for study materials. Second, they lend themselves well to adjustable desk heights.

● ROLLTOP DESK: A study unit that features a flexible top of parallel slats that slide up and down, a rolltop desk provides a convenient enclosure for projects that need to be left undisturbed. More expensive than a standard model, a rolltop is larger than many other styles; consequently, its use is hindered in a small setting. One way to incorporate the look in confined quarters is via custom carpentry, scaling the rolltop down to the study area's exact measurements. One example of this is featured in Chapter 5 on page 83.

Besides wood, desks are available in several materials, from iron to wicker to colorful laminate. The latter is particularly advantageous in a child's room because of its waterproof surface and color possibilities.

An excellent material to consider for a custom desk, laminate affords much convertibility in a unit designed with a reversible top, allowing the user to flip sides for a totally new look in a different color.

Budget-minded shoppers might also consider laminate a good option as a study surface that can rest on storage cubes or file cabinets. Add casters to the latter and create a movable work station.

If more than one child occupies a room, be sure to provide each with a place to study. It's important for those involved in the learning process to have their own special place to work undisturbed. In a setting with little opportunity for privacy, a separate desk may be the only refuge from another person.

In a situation catering to two roommates, remember to forgo side-by-side desk activities if children are at an age where this would be counterproductive. Instead, place each work surface back to back to eliminate distraction between people in close proximity and to provide the feeling of privacy in a shared environment.

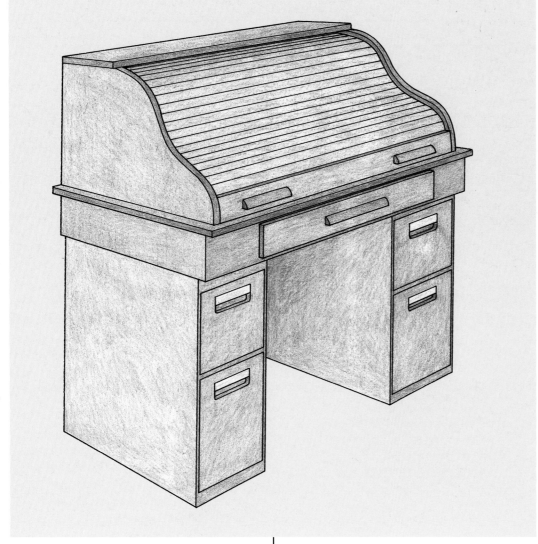

Projects can remain undisturbed in rolltop desks.

COMFORTABLE SEATING

Outfitting a growing student for home study doesn't have to mean a short-lived seating purchase. There are several options that allow for growth spurts. Allow your child the opportunity to test a few while furniture shopping, letting comfort and construction guide your selection as much as cost and convertibility factors. Listed in alphabetical order, some of them follow.

• FOLDING METAL CHAIR: An ideal candidate for auxiliary seating because it tucks away in small spaces, a folding metal chair works well in settings where space is at a premium or where short-

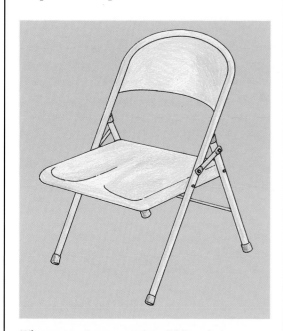

Where space is at a premium, folding chairs enable tuck away when not in use.

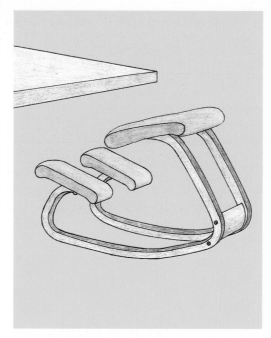

Alternative seating like Scandinavian "Balans" chairs contour to the human anatomy.

term tasks are the rule rather than the exception. Bright colors can complement children's decor, while price is appealing to any budget. The main detriment to this kind of seating is its lack of comfort as a long-term study chair. A seat cushion may be added for more comfort.

Two other considerations: Folding chairs can be repainted easily, adding to their convertibility aspect. They are the perfect complement to a folding table in a room where special projects often require a spare surface on a temporary basis.

• SCANDINAVIAN "BALANS" CHAIR: Devised in Norway as an alternative seating system that would eliminate back strain by contouring to the human anatomy, the Balans chair is uniquely shaped seating meant to be rested "on" not "in." Available through Scandinavian furniture stores, it allows your body to relax in a position of natural balance and good posture with minimal use of muscles. Proponents claim better circulation and breathing are possible using them. Made in many designs, the most popular is a backless version with a knee rest on a base that either rocks or remains stationary, adjusting to different heights.

• SECRETARIAL CHAIR: Perhaps the most adaptable desk chair from the

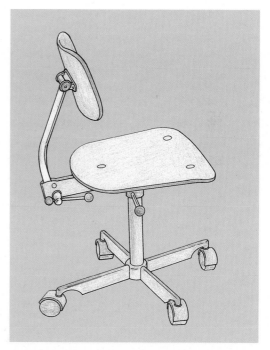

Secretarial chairs afford adaptability in height and position because of adjustable seats and back rests.

standpoint of accommodating different heights and postures, secretarial seating is used in most business offices. Made with an adjustable seat and back, it features legs on casters and therefore offers mobility. Although available in a variety of upholstery fabrics, this kind of chair also comes in wood or covered in vinyl, which may be more practical for child use.

• STRAIGHT-BACK CHAIR: The most common kind of chair teamed with a desk, the straight-back chair may look more at home with conventional wood furnishings for study. Besides being uncomfortable to sit on for long periods of

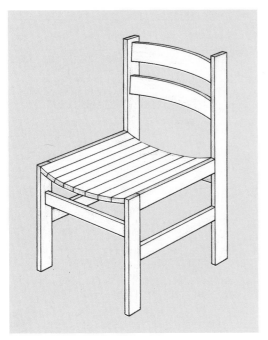

Teamed with a desk, a traditional straight-back chair finds a suitable home.

time, however, its main drawback is its difficulty being moved over carpet. For a young child, this could present a burdensome problem.

Seats built in to the recesses or the bay of a child's bedroom window are a blessing for many reasons. Not only do they provide special storage possibilities for bulk items like sports equipment, but they promote good access to natural light while playing or reading. They also offer instant extra seating for company, usually accommodating more than one person.

Window seats have another advantage over other kinds of seating: they serve as an ideal resting place for play pals like dolls and stuffed animals.

GOOD LIGHTING

With proper lighting, a child's bedroom can become the right place for playing, reading, studying and pursuing other everyday activities.

Before deciding what kind of fixture to buy, determine what you want light to accomplish in the room. To best evaluate your child's needs, consider the three basic kinds of artificial illumination:

• GENERAL LIGHTING: General lighting should provide comfortable background brightness, reducing shadows and contributing to overall environmental well-being. Accomplish this by providing an atmosphere where light is reflected from walls, ceiling or large sources overhead.

• TASK LIGHTING: Task lighting should supply localized illumination for specific activities such as writing, reading and doing projects. The entire task area should be illuminated in such a way that shadows are at a minimum.

• ACCENT LIGHTING: Accent lighting should dramatize the focal points in a space. A treasured doll collection. A special wall hanging. A prized picture. Any of these might deserve individual accent light. Primarily a decorative ploy, it should be used in conjunction with task and general lighting. An accent light on a significant item might also perform the added function of serving as a childhood beacon at night.

Although energy conservation and rising electricity costs dictate getting the most for your money, they should not be all you consider before investing in a fixture. Keep in mind that while good lighting can create a stimulating atmosphere, bad lighting can do just the opposite, frustrating someone doing even simple tasks.

A trip to the lighting store should be preceded by a thorough examination of the room your child occupies. If the color scheme is light, realize that whatever illumination you provide will reflect light colors, making a room seem larger. Conversely, if a room color scheme is dark, it will tend to absorb light, making the room look smaller.

Regardless of the kind of lighting chosen, it should never be glaring. To prevent this, avoid using fixtures with bulbs in direct view. Again, light reflected from walls and

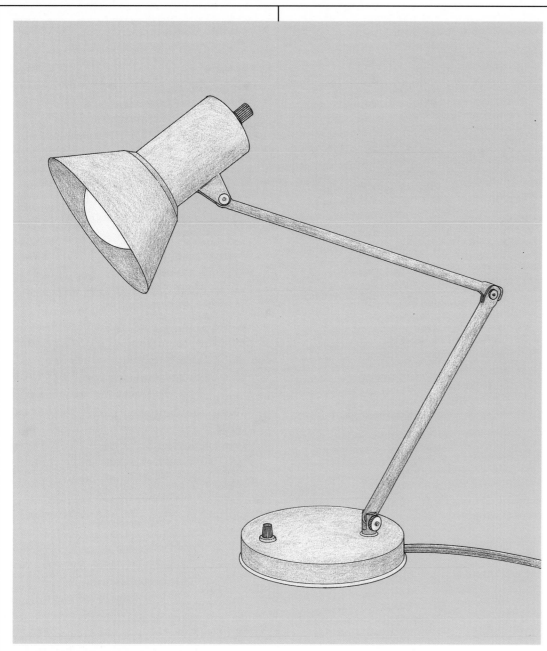

Task lights supply localized illumination for reading, writing and other projects that require concentrated light.

ceiling give the least glare, creating comfortable visible surroundings.

The effect, style and size of a light all determine the fixture best suited to your needs. Of the many types available, the following are the most commonly used in children's bedrooms. They are listed in alphabetical order.

● CLIP-ON LIGHTS: Offering illumination on a moment's notice anywhere it's needed, a clip-on light requires a shelf, the edge of a desk or a headboard or any similar surface to be secured. Available in both gooseneck and swivel styles, they are very reasonably priced. Before investing in one, however, check to be certain that the clamp provides a firm grip to prevent the possibility of a fire hazard from a fallen fixture.

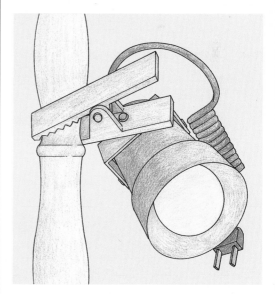

Clip-on lights offer illumination in tight spots where other fixtures don't always fit.

● DIMMER-CONTROLLED LIGHT: A dimmer-controlled fixture raises or lowers the lighting level to varied intensities. It can transform a child's bright bedroom into a special serene kingdom at the flick of a finger. Like magic to a young one, a dimmer can provide the proper mood for special activities like puppet shows or private sessions spent listening to music.

Raise or lower the lighting intensity with dimmer-controlled fixtures that help create special moods.

One other consideration: Dimmer switches differ. Some turn on to a full hand twist, others to the flick of a finger. Check on the method that works best for your child, realizing hand-grasp limitations of the very young.

● FLASHLIGHTS: Portable lights offer young sleepers additional security in the middle of the night or in case of a power failure. Be sure to check the batteries periodically so there are no unpleasant surprises when the lights go out!

● TRACK LIGHTS: The most versatile system available, track lights allow limitless illumination effects. Each metal track contains a continuous electrical circuit so that fixtures can be positioned easily anywhere along the track. Literally enabling you to direct light where you want it, track lighting can be either mounted, suspended or recessed into a ceiling or wall. Tracks can be arranged in lines, T-formations, squares or other patterns to suit your tastes and needs. To bring illumination down to child level, use light fixtures on retractable cords like the kind in Allison's own room pictured on pages 54 and 57. Attached to ceiling-mounted criss-crossed tracks, they were adjustable by simply pulling the shade up or down. (This same versatility can be achieved with a single ceiling-mounted light and retractable cord mechanism. Stores carrying Scandinavian furnishings often carry this style of lighting.)

Remember: More than one fixture on a track means more than one light source

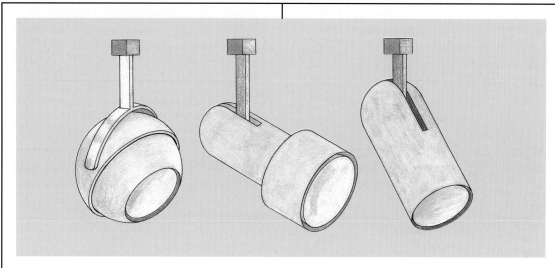

Direct light wherever you want with adjustable track fixtures.

using energy. Be aware of the power drain tracks can have. To combat high energy usage in a child's room, add a dimmer to the track system there.

LIGHT BULBS

Just as important as the fixture you buy is the bulb you put into it. In most cases, regular incandescent bulbs suffice, but don't take that for granted. It's wise to pay attention to wattage requirements so you get the proper illumination. The intensity varies depending on the type of fixture, bulb, wattage and safety precautions.

Fluorescent bulbs may be another option, if not in a child's bedroom perhaps in a playroom illuminated by such fixtures. Although readily available and inexpensive, think twice before investing in them. Much more desirable are full-spectrum

lights described in Chapter 3. Made to duplicate as nearly as possible the natural spectrum of outdoor sunlight, these kinds of fixtures are an all-purpose white light, enabling those illuminated by them to see black and white more distinctly and sharply than ordinary fluorescents. Colors and other details are also visible in truer and more accurate form. But what makes them even more desirable is their ability to cut down on fatigue and eyestrain, common complaints of fluorescent light users.

Providing a child's developing eyes with sufficient illumination is the bottom line on good lighting. So crucial is this to good health, it isn't worth cutting corners. Spotlights provide focused light on specific areas, while floodlights create overall light in a general area. Three-way bulbs provide different levels of illumination as needed.

The only frivolous side to this subject involves periodic use of colored bulbs

tied in to a child's chromatic preferences. Although not the best illumination to read by, colored light bulbs supply a quick change of environment. Not only a playful alternative once in a while, variegated bulbs are a very inexpensive way to alter a room's look when a special mood is desired.

SAFETY TIPS

Because artificial illumination translates to electricity, there are certain precautions worth taking to assure no accidents happen. Make your young one aware of the following:

• Night-lights supply comfort and safety from tripping in the dark, but be sure no sleepy reader plops a book or anything else over one that could cause a fire.

• Closet lights, especially in storage space converted to a special haven, provide needed illumination but also demand careful attention to placement. To prevent the possibility of burning fabric, mount any fixture at least eighteen inches from clothing or other stored items.

• Unused plugs, especially in rooms catering to the very young, should be capped off with outlet covers as a precaution.

• To avoid the possibility of tripping, electric cords on floor lamps should be placed out of the way or gathered and taped to eliminate excess.

• Don't overload an outlet with too many lights or other electric items.

FLOOR COVERING

A child's floor covering could provide as much cuddly reassurance as a comfy bed. Whether playing games or listening to music while stretched on the floor, it's always more comfortable to spread out on a softly textured surface.

Besides choice, color is the most important aspect of any floor covering. Because of the surface it occupies, floor treatment has the greatest impact in a room next to walls. By allowing a child to determine what color will be underfoot, you add to his or her view of the space as "mine."

Deciding what kind of floor covering to place in a child's room depends not only on the age of the child but on the main activities in which he's absorbed. A budding ballet dancer won't benefit from a floor covered in wall-to-wall carpeting, nor will an avid toy car collector enjoy maneuvering his machines across a tufted surface.

In many children's rooms, the best floor treatment is a mix of vinyl and fiber. Just because one area of a room needs to be free of carpeting by virtue of activities staged there, doesn't mean the rest of the space requires the same treatment. Simply divide the territory into separate sections, adding a softer look in one area, a smoother look in another. That way a child can pursue painting and other messy pursuits on a spill-repellent surface and enjoy less accident-prone pastimes on textured surfaces.

Good options for younger children are area rugs of the bathroom mat variety. They are not only a reasonable and handy solution to the floor covering problem, but they are easily washable when soiled.

Older children, who don't give the floor as heavy a workout, may be ideal candidates for wall-to-wall carpeting. Because price per square yard varies considerably, shop around, asking reputable retailers to familiarize you with construction and wearability features. Instead of a plush thickness, you might consider a denser commercial-type carpeting. Toys and casters move more easily on a commercial carpet surface, which is easier to maintain than some thicker piles.

Beware of unbelievable bargains. Carpeting is just like anything else—you get what you pay for. Cheap carpet that wears out quickly may cost more in the long run when you consider replacement price.

One other word of caution: Don't be swayed by a sales pitch touting patterned carpet designs as a way to disguise spots and stains. These kinds of floor coverings create very busy environments for young ones and visually close in their corner of the world.

WALL COVERINGS

Paint, fabric and wallpaper. Those are the alternative wall treatments in a child's room.

As previously discussed in detail, a child should pick the palette that will color his or her personal quarters. Without question, paint is the least expensive means of providing color to walls and ceiling. To determine the right shade for the room in question, let your child first see a preferred color in a range of paint chips from pastel to primary. Next, try several large patches of color samples on the actual surface to be covered, realizing that a color viewed on a paint chart or a paint chip will change dramatically when applied to a large area. Before placing a paint order, buy quart-size cans of several colors in close proximity in the spectrum. That way, a few can be tested on a wall before a child makes the final choice with parental approval.

Proper color isn't the only factor to consider when picking paint. It's important to decide what kind of finish should be applied to a particular surface. Depending on whether you want a dull or shiny look, you'll need to opt for either flat or glossy paint.

Latex, or water-based paint, provides a flat finish that is adequate for covering bedroom walls and ceilings. Be aware that flat paint absorbs light, creating the illusion of a larger room. Glossy, or oil-based paint, on the other hand, reflects light, tending to close in a room visually by making the walls appear closer together than they really are.

The best solution in most rooms is a combination of flat and glossy. While flat latex paint does a good job on walls and ceilings, glossy paint is preferable on doors, window frames and shelves, which require a tougher treatment that protects the finish. Keep in mind that glossy surfaces can be wiped clean of dirty fingerprints and stains, while flat surfaces cannot without removing some of the paint.

A more decorative way of treating a child's room is wall covering either in ready-made papers or vinyls that come pre-pasted or not. Swatches of patterns fill thousands of books available at most paint and some hardware stores. Many books devote themselves to children's environments. Be careful not to select something that caters to your taste instead of your child's. To help in the decision, order a sample six-foot strip if possible.

Be mindful of theme papers that time-lock a room. If a child has his heart set on a particular theme, suggest localizing it to one wall.

Before attempting to hang any paper, familiarize yourself with proper application and wall preparation techniques.

In a room two children share, treating walls in paper or vinyl coverings can be tricky. Parental guidance plays a key role here in coordinating the choices both pick. The best way to incorporate two different patterns might be by allowing each child to pick one wall as personal territory.

Besides paint and rolls of wall covering, there are other ways to detail a child's room. Borders offer an attractive alternative that can help bring the height of the room down to a child's level. They can be achieved either by painting a design, like a stripe or a decoration such as Allison's

dancing carrots, that circumscribes the room, or applying a wallpaper border. Generally speaking, I recommend placing borders one foot above the child's current height; however, if this placement would interrupt light switches or fight with the architecture of the space, then raise or lower the ornamental strip a few inches to avoid the problem.

Fantasy artwork in the form of murals or other designs also are a way of decorating a child's space. But don't fall into the trap of creating a fantasy room for someone who will soon outgrow it. If this technique appeals to your young one, keep it simple. Clouds. Stars. Sun. Moon. Any of them might have a place in your child's design scheme, just as a rainbow did in young Michael's domain.

WALL HANGINGS

Artwork in a child's room need not be elaborate. Very young children enjoy seeing their own imaginative creations in a prominent place. When framed, these one-of-a-kind works offer a delightful reflection of a budding artist's flights of fancy.

Paper cutouts of the human form or a child's name are also ideal personal touches for living spaces that address the young. An inexpensive way to provide decoration, such cutouts are ideal parent/child projects.

Older children tend to prefer posters and pictures of pop figures and other celebrities. They might also select personal

photographs as wall hangings. If their artistic collection presents display problems on an ordinary wall surface, entertain the idea of a corkboard wall, bulletin board or the back of a door. One other advantage of a corkboard wall is its sound absorption.

A bulletin board can also be beneficial for a young child as a nonverbal communication center that does double duty as a decorative element.

Pictures and photos aren't the only decorations to consider as wall hangings. Personal treasures such as baseball batting caps, trophies and car models might be ideal displayed on walls.

Although it may not be the best idea in a room occupied by someone with occasional sticky fingers, fabric on stretched frames might be another alternative to wall art. Older children enjoy this kind of application because of its textural qualities. Fabric also has the benefit of being able to tie in an overall look so that bed, window and wall coverings match.

Still other ideas for wall hangings include a simple calendar or clock, or possibly a row of decorative coat hooks.

Always make sure, however, that the wall hanging is placed at your child's height. Young eyes that have to strain to see something too high on their walls won't benefit from the experience.

WINDOW COVERINGS

Window coverings not only provide a decorative element in a child's room set-

Mini-blinds let light filter in through strips of metal, wood or plastic.

ting but also offer some privacy from the outside world. Accessibility plays a vital role here since small hands need to be able to manipulate window coverings easily from their vantage point.

As you consider different window treatments, keep in mind the necessity for darkness in a child's room at naptime and bedtime. See-through coverings may look good but defeat the purpose of a good night's—or a good day's—sleep. Lining window fabric also prevents sun damage.

Like anything else, the cost of window

coverings varies according to materials and complexity of construction. The following ideas, listed in alphabetical order, run the gamut from cheap to expensive.

● BLINDS: Strips of metal or wood that obscure light, blinds are reasonable resources for window coverings. One advantage they have over many other designs is availability in multiple colors. Sometimes, they can be ordered in reversible colors or stripes.

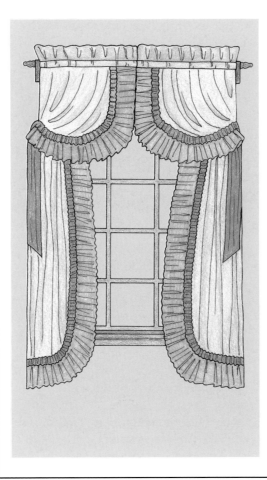

● CURTAINS: Window treatments that can be drawn up or sideways, curtains are an inexpensive way to decorate. Resist any urge to purchase frilly designs since they may end up in disarray if maintenance depends on a young occupant's care and concern.

● DRAPERIES: Although fabric that drapes a window can do an ideal job blocking out light and keeping out cold, it might be too much for small hands to

Frilly curtains offer many fanciful possibilities in children's rooms but their care may prohibit practicality.

maneuver because of fabric weight. However, draperies can tie a room's look together very well by complementing other material.

● GREENHOUSES: Miniature greenhouses that fit into window frames and usually are shaped in a bay design offer an interesting alternative, especially in the room of a budding gardener or pet lover. Be careful sunlight is not too intense for any living creature, or consider having the glass tinted to cut down on the sun's rays. Also take care to select a model featuring ventilation. Those who opt for this more costly kind of window treatment should still consider a covering to block out light from the interior of the room.

● PAPER SHADES: Another inexpensive way to decorate, paper shades pull down on a roll secured to the top of a window. They allow light to fill the room and come in varied colors as well as rice paper.

● ROMAN SHADES: Folding like a pleated accordion, Roman shades are an ideal solution in a child's room. Because they're adjustable, they provide varied light possibilities. They also can unify a look by coordinating with other room fabrics. Your child may find a Roman shade easier to use if it's mounted on the window sill and lifted by a simple pulley system.

Greenhouse windows solve light, ventilation and space concerns for budding gardeners.

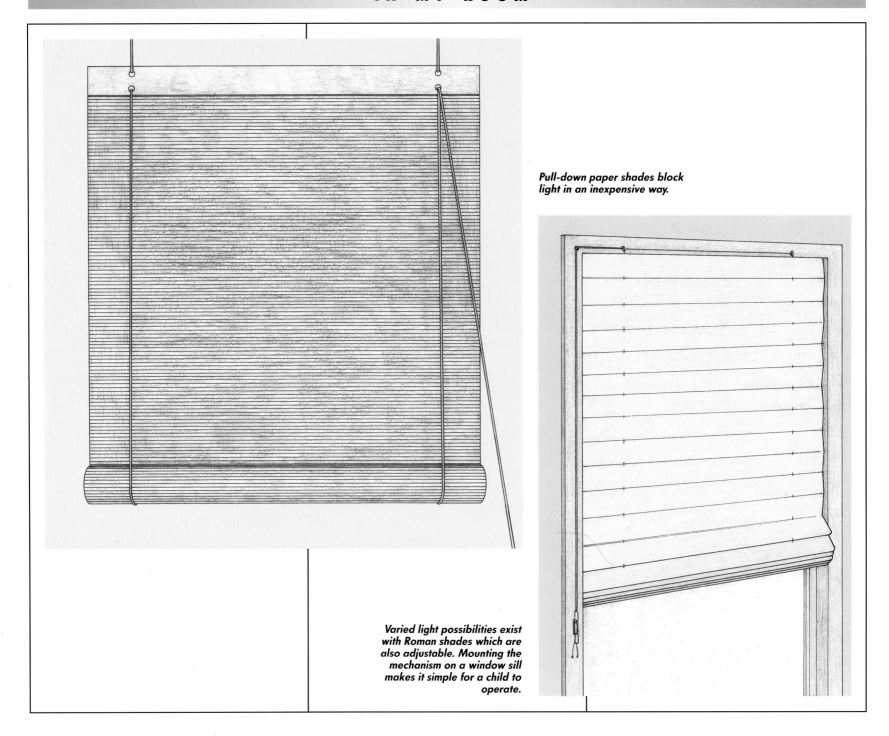

Pull-down paper shades block light in an inexpensive way.

Varied light possibilities exist with Roman shades which are also adjustable. Mounting the mechanism on a window sill makes it simple for a child to operate.

Shutters with movable louvers afford many ways to control light.

● SHUTTERS: Window coverings with fitted movable louvers, shutters do an excellent job of controlling light. Available in natural wood or in custom colors, they are more expensive than many other treatments, although less expensive ready-made versions are on the market. Depending on the quality purchased, shutters can be long-lasting and durable.

No matter what kind of window treatment you consider, keep in mind it will be visible from the outside. Because of that, you may want to limit your choices of color and pattern. Also be aware that sunlight eventually fades and deteriorates material, so you may want to protect certain fabric investments by shielding them from harsh rays with shades that block out the light.

DESIGNS FOR THE DISABLED

In a room for a disabled child, there are several considerations worthy of attention before decorating begins. Cabinets, shelves and other storage units should be easily adjustable to accommodate special needs. Those confined to a wheelchair deserve attention to how easily that piece of equipment can be maneuvered through the room. Perhaps the best study surface for someone in this situation is a desktop that slides out over the lap, eliminating the need to scoot underneath it.

Although costly, custom design is well worth considering in a room for a disabled

A MATTER OF BUDGET

What can you afford to do in a child's room with a limited budget?
Are there any custom features a medium budget will allow?
What are the ramifications of a sky's-the-limit expense account?

Answers to all these questions depend on how little or how much money can be invested in a project. The following chart serves as a guide, with categories delineated in alphabetical order. Essential acquisitions have not been repeated in higher classifications which list conceivable additions or new treatments altogether.

	LOW	MEDIUM	HIGH
ACCESSORIES:	Bulletin board; Wastebasket; Desk essentials	Coordinated fabrics; Learning tools	Custom or decorator fabrics; Quality collectibles
ART:	Child's own art	Poster prints	Framed art
CLOSET:	Accessible rods at child height	Simple conversion to hideaway loft or puppet theater or clothes storage facility	Total renovation as extra room for study, etc.
FABRICS:	Throw pillows; Covered bulletin board; Lamp shades	Coordinated bedcovers and curtains	Custom-designed fabric treatments
FLOOR COVERING:	Partial floor treatment with indoor/outdoor carpet; Bath mats; Sample cuttings; Remnants; Plastic drop cloth for spills	Complete floor treatment with wall-to-wall carpet; Linoleum for spill areas; Handmade rugs like imported dhurries	Custom colors and fibers; Custom-designed rugs or carpets
FURNITURE:	Bed; Desk with chair; Storage units	Coordinated suite of laminated or wood furniture	Custom designs, e.g., bed with built-in bookcase on headboard
LIGHTING:	Night-light; Task lights by desk and bed	Track lights	Custom and neon lights
PAINT:	Standard colors	Custom colors	Murals and faux finishes
WALL COVERS:	Stencil patterns; Stripes or dado borders	Quality vinyls and wallpapers; Special borders	Fantasy applications
WINDOW COVERS:	Pull-down shades; Mini-blinds	Custom blinds; Roman shades; Shutters	Custom window fabrics; Greenhouse window box

child. Furniture that doesn't fight any specific challenge can make all the difference in the world. If you choose this route, make certain to take as much care with hardware as with design. Not all knobs and drawer pulls are easy to grasp for young ones, especially those with special needs.

Parents of children confined to wheelchairs also should pay close attention to that piece of equipment. Just because it's a part of the construction, don't assume that the accompanying cushion is comfortable or as longlasting as the chair itself. Be sure to check periodically to see if it's time for a

SHOPPING WITH FORESIGHT

Anxious as you and your young one may be to complete a decorating project, exercise restraint as you shop around. Better to be satisfied with something that took longer to find than to make do with an inferior choice purchased in haste.

One way to help prevent mistakes is to measure space requirements, taking them on a shopping expedition along with a copy of the Master Plan and any sample swatches you might have. Second-guessing figures, fabric and paint colors is a no-win situation.

A WORD TO THE WISE

As in all aspects of a child's living space, cleanup materials should be close at hand in case of spills and other accidents. Maintenance should always be a priority in this setting, whether pertaining to the space itself or to personal effects.

Assign an area for a hamper or some other dirty clothes container. Base the location on easy accessibility for a child but not so close that unpleasant laundry odors permeate the room. If there's a water play space, an area for wet, soiled items should be provided.

Yet another area should be devoted to necessary tools for keeping a living environment clean. Feather dusters, rubber gloves, a dustpan and broom, clothespins and clean rags should be stored there.

A FINAL MESSAGE

Nurturing a child doesn't only mean providing proper food and care and clothing. It also means providing shelter that caters to personal needs.

There is no better way to prepare a young one for the outside world than to allow self-discovery in a setting that reflects a growing mind and growing tastes. Just as the cave man proved with his primitive markings, the need to make a personal imprint in the space we occupy exists in us all.

CHAPTER 8

Childhood interests follow as many pathways as a growing mind allows.

- A ballet bar for a budding dancer.
- A canvas stage for a young puppeteer.
- A wood bin for an aspiring carpenter.
- A personal home computer for a deaf boy.

Learning centers stimulate young minds. These areas foster interest in preferred pastimes and channel childhood curiosity in a new direction.

Helping young ones to develop by permitting specialized work stations within their reach is an excellent way to encourage new discoveries. The tools to make these interest areas come alive need not be costly. Often, your search can begin and end in the Great Outdoors. Nature objects like rocks and shells, leaves and nests may offer just as much intrigue as fancy equipment from specialty stores.

Another often overlooked resource for learning center materials is the household cupboard stocked with materials fascinating to young minds. Empty milk cartons, clothespins and aluminum foil are just a few "finds" that children consider appealing enough to incorporate in their every day play world.

A Place for Learning

"A discovery, to be real, must contain something new. This element of novelty is an open door to those who have the courage to go through."

—Dr. Maria Montessori,
The Formation of Man

Although the ones spending time at these special work and play stations should cast the deciding vote about their makeup, there are some pointers to consider when creating them.

Creating centers in a child's room that foster learning takes more than time and energy. To ensure success, it also takes careful thought, planning and guidance.

Communication is the key to this entire concept. Whether it's a playroom or a personal bedroom, let a child tell you how he or she envisions that space.

Before taking any steps, consider the following:

- Narrow the number of learning centers to a child's most important interests, paying attention to the ones carried back and forth to school.

- Never force an activity on a child that he or she isn't yet interested in pursuing.

- Keep an open mind about the number of activities that may interest a child. One or two learning centers supplying hours of entertainment and discovery are better than a half dozen stifling creativity and generating wasted time.

- Not every childhood interest belongs indoors. Kickball is a good example of a pastime that has no place in some confined areas.

- Safety first is a good rule to follow before devoting space to certain leisure activities. Pastimes potentially dangerous, like bows and arrows or darts, might not belong in a setting a young one will occupy.

What follows is a list of exciting childhood interests and pertinent information about them. Meant to serve as a guide, they are just a sampling of what could rate learning center status in your child's room.

ART

□ GOAL To foster creative expression, allowing a child to fabricate images of the world as he or she sees it.

□ LOCATION Anywhere in a room except areas near clothes, fabrics or bedding.

□ LEARNING TOOLS Be imaginative! Include basic items such as pencils, marker pens, crayons, chalk, watercolors, poster paints, other pigments, fingerpaints, craft paper, drawing pads, poster board, canvas, easels and brushes.

□ OTHER EQUIPMENT Smocks, aprons, cleanup materials, paper towels and clean rags.

□ SPECIAL CONSIDERATION Plastic drop cloths or a piece of linoleum should be placed on top of the work surface to ensure safety from wet materials like watercolors. Spill-free containers should be used when possible.

□ FINAL NOTE Framing artwork and using it as decor is one of the finest ways of placing a child's *signature* in an environment and promoting a positive self-image.

BUILDING BLOCKS

□ GOAL To develop eye/hand coordination, an understanding of geometric shapes and the development of building skills, math principles and constructive play.

□ LOCATION Floor space or tabletop surface.

□ LEARNING TOOLS Any plastic, cardboard, fabric or wooden block forms; for more advanced children, high-tech building games.

□ SPECIAL CONSIDERATION Storing items might require special drawers or containers.

CLEANUP

□ GOAL To teach room maintenance and orderliness in an enjoyable way.

□ LOCATION Anywhere space will allow including a wall surface.

□ LEARNING TOOLS Wastebasket, dustpan, dust brushes, dust cloths, mops, brooms, sponges, rags and rubber gloves.

□ SPECIAL CONSIDERATION Avoid using toxic cleansers and be sure to provide household tools scaled down to a child's size.

COLLECTIONS

☐ GOAL · To encourage care of fine things.

☐ LOCATION · Shelves.

☐ LEARNING TOOLS · Dolls, stuffed animals, figurines, awards and trophies.

☐ SPECIAL CONSIDERATION · Expensive collections might be better kept behind glass or in an enclosure free of dust and soil.

COMPUTERS

☐ GOAL · To teach computer skills and auxiliary learning.

☐ LOCATION · A desktop near appropriate outlets with sufficient work surfaces in close proximity.

☐ LEARNING TOOLS · Personal home computer, periphery hardware and software, manuals and boxed paper.

☐ SPECIAL CONSIDERATION · Surfaces should be kept dry and free of magnetized objects. Good lighting should be nearby. Care should be taken to avoid power loss.

CRAFTS

☐ GOAL · To foster creative expression and to give a child a sense of start, middle and finish to a project; to demonstrate how ordinary materials can serve as a basis for creativity.

☐ LOCATION · Tabletop surface.

☐ LEARNING TOOLS · Any of thousands of household items plus craft store supplies such as scissors, glue, tape, pencils, rulers and clay.

☐ SPECIAL CONSIDERATION · Work surfaces should be protected to avoid possibility of damage from glue and other spillables. There should be space for drying projects and cleanup materials.

DANCE

☐ GOAL — To foster creative expression through physical activity and mind/body connection.

☐ LOCATION — Floor space and a wall free to handle some equipment.

☐ LEARNING TOOLS — Large mirror, wall-mounted ballet bar, floor mats, proper footwear, costumes.

☐ SPECIAL CONSIDERATION — For some children, soft surfaces are appropriate; for others, carpeting that can be rolled back or moved away is essential to perform certain dances. This area might be a part of the music center.

DOLLS AND OTHER STUFFED PLAY PALS

☐ GOAL — To encourage fantasy play and companionship.

☐ LOCATION — Anywhere appropriate, from bed to closets.

☐ LEARNING TOOLS — Doll friends and stuffed play characters.

☐ SPECIAL CONSIDERATION — Appropriate storage such as a toy chest with a safety-latch lid.

EXERCISE

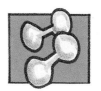

☐ GOAL — To promote a positive self-image and mind/body connection and to provide a means of venting frustrations.

☐ LOCATION — Floor space or specially designed locations.

☐ LEARNING TOOLS — Special equipment including tumble mat, slant board, weights, chinning bar, punching bag and indoor slide.

☐ SPECIAL CONSIDERATION — No sharp-edged furniture should be nearby. All equipment should be safety-checked before using.

FANTASY PLAY

☐ GOAL — To foster constructive fantasy, spontaneous creativity, time for make-believe or space for thought.

☐ LOCATION — Anywhere in the room, including the closet.

☐ LEARNING TOOLS — Dress-up costumes, uniforms, makeup, masks, play jewelry, mirror, storage containers. One option might be a child-size kitchen equipped with play dishes and appliances, or a play house fabricated from a cloth-draped card table.

☐ SPECIAL CONSIDERATION — Avoid designing an entire room around a fantasy or encouraging a room that becomes a total "escape hatch."

THE GALLERY

☐ GOAL — To organize "pop" art, fad items, photographs and other memorabilia into a localized area.

☐ LOCATION — Walls, backs of doors.

☐ LEARNING TOOLS — Posters, photographs, prints, pennants. Cork or fabric walls, push pins, tacks.

☐ SPECIAL CONSIDERATION — Surfaces able to handle adhesives and other securing devices for hanging objects.

LIVING THINGS
(PETS AND PLANTS)

☐ GOAL — To teach children about growth and life as well as death and dying, and to show the living mysteries of the world.

☐ LOCATION — Well-ventilated safe areas away from radiators, heaters and other harmful devices.

☐ LEARNING TOOLS — Animals, plants, bird feeders, window gardens, aquariums, etc.

☐ SPECIAL CONSIDERATION — Waterproof surfaces easily maintained. Cleanliness, fresh food, air and water are essential.

MUSIC

☐ GOAL — To promote sound association and music appreciation.

☐ LOCATION — Any appropriate area, possibly near electric outlets.

☐ LEARNING TOOLS — Records, record player, tapes, tape recorder, musical instruments, handmade noisemakers.

☐ SPECIAL CONSIDERATION — Storage capabilities and sound absorption, if necessary.

NON-VERBAL

☐ GOAL — To provide a message center as a means of non-verbal communication between parent and child, or child and siblings.

☐ LOCATION — Wall surfaces or backs of doors.

☐ LEARNING TOOLS — Bulletin board and markers and/or clipboard and paper and/or chalkboard, chalk and eraser.

☐ SPECIAL CONSIDERATION — Be careful of push pins, tacks, etc. Avoid using the entrance door.

PERSONAL GROOMING

☐ GOAL — To instill self-pride and personal hygiene habits.

☐ LOCATION — Tabletop or dresser in a bedroom or the bath.

☐ LEARNING TOOLS — Grooming accessories, including combs, brushes, mirror, hair dryers, makeup, perfume, toiletries, nail clippers, etc.

☐ SPECIAL CONSIDERATION — Surface should be durable enough to absorb spills. Be mindful of a child who isn't mature enough to use items such as scissors and toiletries safely.

PUPPET THEATER

☐ GOAL To encourage speech and language skills, fantasy play and descriptive storytelling.

☐ LOCATION Closets, doorways or a freestanding area.

☐ LEARNING TOOLS Hand puppets and hand-made canvas or vinyl panels or a ready-made puppet stage.

☐ SPECIAL CONSIDERATION Stage material should be pliable enough to cut various openings that can accommodate small hands and puppets. Extra backdrops might be considered to create varied stage settings.

PUZZLES AND GAMES

☐ GOAL To provide enjoyment and possibly promote skills inherent to each activity.

☐ LOCATION Tabletop surface, floor or sleeping surfaces.

☐ LEARNING TOOLS Wooden or cardboard puzzles or countless boxed board games.

☐ SPECIAL CONSIDERATION Orderly storage within reach of young ones.

READING

☐ GOAL To develop reading skills including word association.

☐ LOCATION Anywhere appropriate including a desk, the floor or a bed.

☐ LEARNING TOOLS A library of books and other reading materials.

☐ SPECIAL CONSIDERATION Good lighting, comfort-able seating and quiet space.

SCIENCE

☐ GOAL — To encourage the study of nature's mysteries.

☐ LOCATION — Any appropriate place that can accommodate equipment, tools, etc.

☐ LEARNING TOOLS — Items that foster scientific adventures including finds from nature walks or trips to the planetarium or other sources. Consider compasses, clocks, globes and relief maps.

☐ SPECIAL CONSIDERATION — Protected tabletops and other work areas are important as well as proximity to electric outlets. Chemicals require good ventilation. Some scientific studies may also necessitate exposure to sun and fresh air. Be sure a child is old enough to handle such adventures.

SENSORY PLAY

☐ GOAL — To encourage awareness of the five senses.

☐ LOCATION — Tabletop surfaces or shelves.

☐ LEARNING TOOLS — Items homemade or store-bought that encourage sight, smell, taste, touch and hearing such as smell jars, sound shakers and textured fabrics.

☐ SPECIAL CONSIDERATION — Be careful that young ones are not exposed to toxic materials.

STAMP AND COIN COLLECTING

☐ GOAL — To instill an appreciation for valuable collectibles and to develop methodical study habits.

☐ LOCATION — Tabletop surface.

☐ LEARNING TOOLS — Stamps, coins, magnifying glass, albums, publications, envelopes and other perfunctory gear.

☐ SPECIAL CONSIDERATION — Work surfaces should be able to remain undisturbed. Clean, dry storage should be provided. Lighting should be good enough for close work.

VIDEO AND TELEVISION

☐ GOAL — To provide access to educational programs.

☐ LOCATION — Tabletop surface or sturdy shelves.

☐ LEARNING TOOLS — Video monitors and TV sets or other related equipment. Video recorders and players and videotapes.

☐ SPECIAL CONSIDERATION — Electricity, storage for tapes, headphones for silent use. Parents should share in the viewing of such materials.

WALLS AND DOORS

☐ GOAL — To encourage hand and arm motor skills while promoting creative expression such as drawing on an art board.

☐ LOCATION — Backs of doors or flat wall surfaces within hand reach.

☐ LEARNING TOOLS — Blackboards, chalk and erasers; magnet boards and magnets; felt boards and felt cutouts; marker boards, erasers and multi-colored markers; clipboards and pads of paper.

☐ SPECIAL CONSIDERATION — Chalkboards leave dust; markers need to be covered; magnets are not recommended for small children.

WEATHER

☐ GOAL — To instill awareness of the seasons and outdoor elemental changes.

☐ LOCATION — Counter tops, walls, windows.

☐ LEARNING TOOLS — Thermometer, barometer, rain gauge, wind meters, wind socks, wind chimes, etc.

☐ SPECIAL CONSIDERATION — Some instruments need exposure to natural elements like sunlight, rain and wind; therefore, proximity to the outside may be crucial.

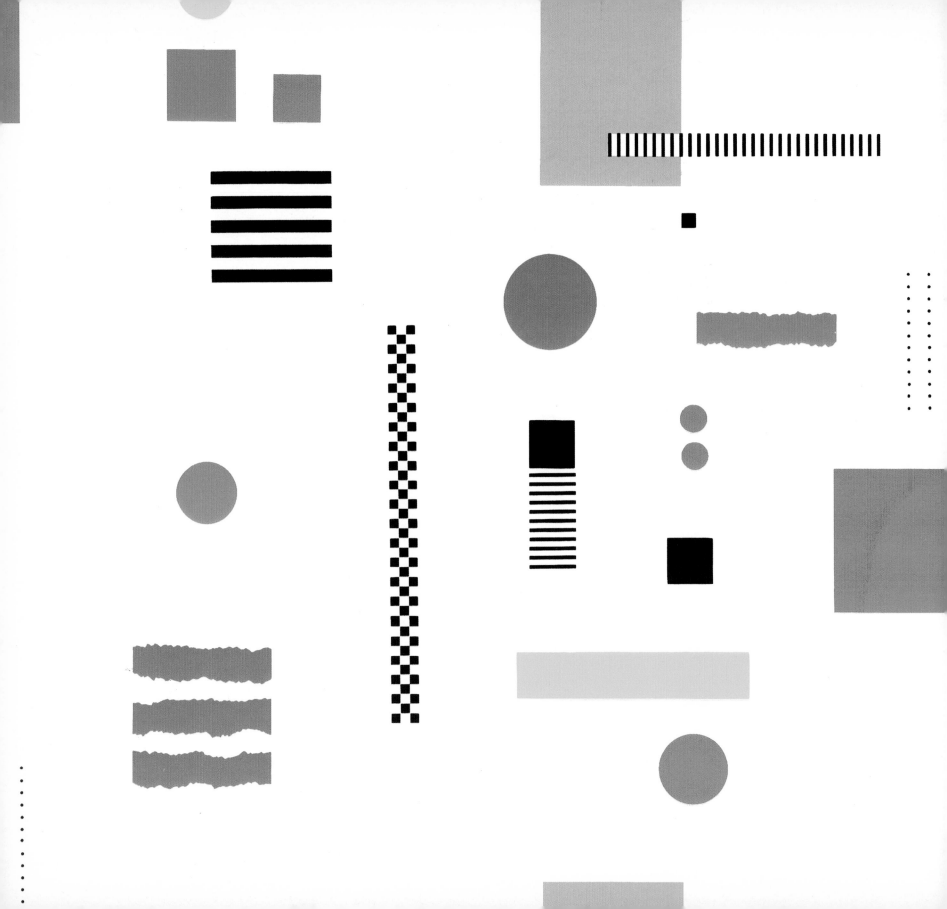

PART · THREE ·

Appendix

The following charts are intended to serve as a standard of measurement for a child in a *living and learning environment*. Strictly guidelines, they have been divided into four categories: Small Child; Average Child; Large-framed Child and the Child in a Wheelchair.

AGES 5–11 YEARS OLD							
	Child Height	Eye-Level (Standing)	Overhead Reach (Standing)	Eye-Level (Sitting)	Overhead Reach (Sitting)	Desk Height	Chair Height
Small Child	40″–45″ / 100–114.3 cm	39.1″ / 99.3 cm	46.6″ / 118.4cm	30.9″ / 78.5cm	—	17.5″ / 44.5cm	10.5″ / 26.7cm
Average Child	46″–48″ / 116.8–121.9cm	43″ / 109.2cm	51.6″ / 131.1cm	33.5″ / 85.1cm	—	19.4″ / 49.3cm	11.5″ / 29.2cm
Large Child	49″–54″ / 124.5–137.2cm	48″ / 121.9cm	57.5″ / 146.1cm	36.9″ / 93.7cm	—	21.4″ / 54.4cm	13″ / 33cm
Child in a Wheelchair	—	—	—	40.8″ / 103.6cm	48.7″ / 123.7cm	31″ / 78.7cm	19.5″ / 49.5cm

SOURCE: Humanscale™ The MIT Press, Cambridge, MA 02142

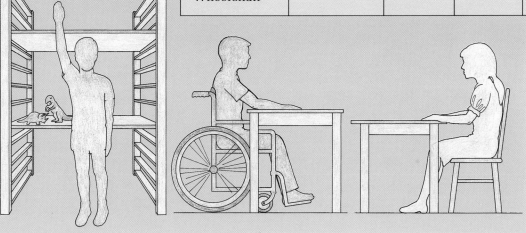

Because any setting should be tailored to the individual for whom it is meant, let the actual measurements of a child dictate the requirements of his or her room when doing a Master Plan.

Glossary of Terms

▼▼▼▼▼▼▼▼▼

BODY PRISM—The human anatomy viewed as a receptor of light.

COLOR—The visual sensation that results from the stimulation of the eye's retina or photoreceptor cells. Red, orange, yellow, green, blue, indigo and violet are the visible colors of the spectrum.

COLOR BLINDNESS—The condition in which an individual's ability to distinguish colors and shades is less than normal.

CONE CELLS—The nerve cells in the eye that help determine the sharpness of vision and the perceived brightness of light. The inability of these cells to transmit color information to the brain is considered the cause of color blindness.

CONVERTIBILITY—The capability of an object or an environment to adapt from one form or use to another.

COORDINATION—The harmonious relationship of muscular activities that allows simple and complex movements.

CORONA DISCHARGES—A ring or crown of light emanating from a luminous body.

DADO—A decorative border circumscribing the walls of a room to raise or lower the visual height of a room. This may be accomplished with paint, wallpaper or other means.

DEUTERANOPES—Color blindness marked by the optic nerve's confusion of red and green.

ELECTROMAGNETIC ENERGY—Energy combining electric and magnetic forces, which include light, heat and radio waves.

FLUORESCENT LIGHT—Illumination emitted from a glass tube coated on the inside with a substance that glows when mercury vapor in the tube is charged by a stream of electrons from the cathode.

FREQUENCY—The number of complete vibrations per second in sound or light waves.

FULL-SPECTRUM LIGHT—An artificial light source that closely resembles the entire spectrum radiated from the sun.

INCANDESCENT LIGHT—Illumination produced from a filament in a lamp charged by electrical current and contained in a glass vacuum. A standard light bulb is a typical example.

INCIDENT LIGHT—Overall general illumination that falls upon an object.

INFRARED—A ray with a wavelength

longer than visible red light. Infrared light is invisible to the eye.

KIRLIAN PHOTOGRAPHY—The process of photographing objects while releasing high-voltage electricity through them at a low amperage thereby capturing on film electromagnetic discharges. It was devised by Semyon and Valentina Kirlian in the 1930s.

LEARNING CENTERS—Specific environments equipped to teach a singular or related series of lessons such as music, art, math and the like.

LIGHT—Radiation capable of stimulating the eye and optic nerve to produce vision. Not all radiation is visible to the human eye such as X-rays, infrared and ultraviolet. The visible spectrum of light includes the colors of the rainbow.

MASTER PLAN—Sketches, drawings and renderings developed in partnership with children as descriptions of their own personal space. This is the first step in designing living and learning environments.

MIND/BODY CONNECTION—The relationship that the mind and body attain when jointly engaged in learning.

MODULAR FURNITURE—Furnishings capable of being stacked, fitted or otherwise rearranged to suit various functions and needs.

MOLECULE—The smallest particle of any element.

MONOECIOUS—Separate male and female reproductive organs existing on the same plant.

MONTESSORI METHOD—The educational theory that teaches young children to learn through self-education and development of the senses as opposed to rigid control of learning activities. Developed by Dr. Maria Montessori in the early 1900s.

MOTOR SKILLS—Muscular movements developed to achieve coordinated responses such as eye/hand coordination and reflexes.

OPTIC NERVE—A pathway to the brain receiving impulses from the retina of the eye.

PERCEPTION—The ability of the senses to comprehend things that are visible, audible, etc.

PHOTOBIOLOGY—The science of studying the relationship of light to health.

PHOTONS—Infinitesimal particles of electromagnetic energy behaving like both particles and waves.

PHOTOSYNTHESIS—The biological creation of chemical compounds by the presence of light. An example of this is the development of chlorophyll in green plants.

PIGMENT—Any matter such as dyes, paints and powders giving color to substances.

PRIMARY COLORS—Red, yellow and blue—the three basic pigment colors from which all other pigment colors may be derived. For light, these are red, green and blue.

PRISM—An object that refracts or bends light thereby spreading it into the visible spectrum. An example is the rainbow of light created from sunlight and raindrops.

PROTONOPES—Color blindness marked by the optic nerve's confusion of red and blue-green.

RADIATION—The movement of rays as light, heat, etc. passing through space as they undergo internal change.

RAINBOW—The dispersion of the sun's rays in falling rain, creating an arc of consecutive bands of color.

RAY—A narrow beam of light and the pathway it follows.

REFLECTED LIGHT—The return of light waves from a surface.

REFRACTED LIGHT—The bending of light waves as they pass from one medium to another.

RETINA—The photo receptor layer of cells located in the back of the eye and sensitive to light. It contains both rods and cones.

RODS—Nerve cells of the retina sensitive to dim light.

ROMAN SHADES—Type of window covering that folds like a pleated accordion and rises or falls by means of a simple rope pulley system.

SECONDARY COLORS—Orange, yellow and purple—the pigment colors derived by mixing two other pigment colors.

SIGNATURES—Personal descriptions and choices children make while imagining their personal environments.

SPECTRUM—A series of colored bands arranged in the order of their respective wavelengths, i.e., red, orange, yellow, green, blue, indigo, violet.

TIME-LAPSE PHOTOGRAPHY—The technique of photographing a slow and continuous process, like plant growth, so that it appears faster when projected at higher speed.

TRITANOPES—Color blindness characterized by seeing the spectrum in tones of red and green.

TRUNDLE BED—A low, rolling bed that fits under another bed when not in use.

ULTRAVIOLET—A ray with a wavelength shorter than that of visible violet light.

VELCRO—A brand of interlocking tape consisting of opposing pieces of fabric, one with tiny nylon hooks and the other with dense nylon pile.

WAVE—A state of motion that advances as it is transmitted from one particle to the next in a given direction such as with light and sound.

WAVELENGTH—The distance between the crest of one wave and the crest of the next.

WHITE LIGHT—The composition of all visible wavelengths of light ranging from red to violet.

Recommended Reading

▼▼▼▼▼▼▼

The following recommended reading list is meant to serve as a resource guide to scientific, educational and environmental information touched upon in this book. By mentioning the following publications, the authors do not endorse any one single theory nor have they received the endorsement of any authors mentioned.

Anderson, Peggy. *Children's Hospital*. New York: Harper & Row, 1985.

Babbitt, Edwin S. *The Principles of Light and Color*. Secaucus, N.J.: Citadel Press, 1967.

Beasley, Victory R., Ph.D. *Your Electro-Vibratory Body*. Boulder Creek, Calif.: University of the Trees Press, 1978.

Becker, Robert O., MD, and Gary Seldon. *The Body Electric: Electromagnetism and the Foundation of Life*. New York: William Morrow, 1985.

Bettelheim, Bruno. *A Good Enough Parent: A Book on Child Rearing*. New York: Alfred A. Knopf, 1987.

Birren, Faber. *Color: A Survey in Words and Pictures*. Secaucus, N.J.: Citadel Press, 1963.

———*Color and Human Response*. New York: Van Nostrand Reinhold, 1978.

———*Color Psychology and Color Therapy*. Secaucus, N.J.: Citadel Press, 1978.

Bloom, Benjamin S. *Developing Talent in Young People*. New York: Ballantine Books, 1985.

Clark, Linda A., M.A. *Color Therapy*. Old Greenwich, Conn.: Devin Adair, 1980.

Dadd, Debra Lynn. *Nontoxic & Natural*. Los Angeles: Jeremy Tarcher, 1984.

Davis, Mikol, and Earle Lane. *Rainbows of Life: The Promise of Kirlian Photography*. New York: Harper & Row, 1978.

de Bono, Edward. *The Dog Exercising Machine*. New York: Simon and Schuster, 1970.

Doman, Glenn. *What to Do About Your Brain-Injured Child*. Garden City, N.Y.: Doubleday, 1974.

Flatow, Ira. *Rainbows, Curve Balls, and Other Wonders of the Natural World Explained*. New York: William Morrow, 1988.

Grainger, Stuart E. *Making Aids for Disabled Living*. London: B.T. Batsford, 1981.

Hale, Glorya. *The Source Book for the Disabled*. London: Imprint Books Limited, 1979.

Hofmann, Ruth B., OTR, BA, RN, BS. *How to Build Special Furniture and Equipment for Handicapped Children*. Springfield, Ill.: Charles C. Thomas, 1970.

Hunt, Roland, *The Seven Keys to Colour Healing.* London: C.W. Daniel, 1977.

Kime, Zane R., MD, MS. *Sunlight.* Penryn, Calif.: World Health Publications, 1980.

Kron, Joan. *Home-Psych.* New York: Clarkson-Potter, 1977.

Lane, Earle. *Electrophotography.* San Francisco: And/Or Press, 1975.

Lifchez, Raymond. *Rethinking Architecture, Design Students and Physically Disabled People.* Berkeley, Calif.: University of California Press, 1987.

Life Library of Photography. *Color.* New York: Time-Life Books, 1970.

Life Library of Photography. *Light and Film.* New York: Time-Life Books, 1970.

Ludington-Hoe, Dr. Susan, with Susan K. Golant. *How to Have a Smarter Baby.* New York: Bantam Books, 1987.

Luscher, Dr. Max. *The Luscher Color Test.* New York: Pocket Books, 1977.

Mander, Jerry. *Four Arguments for the Elimination of Television.* New York: William Morrow, 1977.

Marshall Editions Limited. *Colour.* London: Marshall Editions, 1983.

Montessori, Dr. Maria. *The Absorbent Mind.* New York: Dell Publishing, 1967.

———*The Formation of Man.* London: The Theosophical Publishing House, 1971.

Murphy, Albert T. *Special Children, Special Parents.* Englewood Cliffs, N.J.: Prentice Hall, 1981.

Nordic Committee on Disability. *The More We Do Together: Adapting the Environment for Children with Disabilities.* New York: World Rehabilitation Fund, 1985.

Ott, John N. *Health and Light.* New York: Pocket Books, 1973.

———*Light, Radiation and You: How to Stay Healthy.* Old Greenwich, Conn.: Devin Adair, 1982.

Pearce, Joseph Chilton. *Magical Child.* New York: Bantam Books, 1977.

———*Magical Child Matures.* New York: E. P. Dutton, 1985.

Raschko, Betty Ann. *Housing Interiors for the Disabled and Elderly.* New York: Van Nostrand Reinhold, 1982.

Sommer, Robert. *Personal Space: The Behavioral Basis of Design.* Englewood Cliffs, N.J.: Prentice-Hall, 1969.

Taylor, Anne P., Ph.D., and George Vlastos. *School Zone: Learning Environments for Children.* Grand Haven, Mich.: School Zone Publishing, 1983.

Verny, Thomas, MD, with John Kelly. *The Secret Life of the Unborn Child.* New York: Dell Publishing, 1981.

Weinstein, Carol Simon, and Thomas G. David, eds. *Spaces for Children: The Built Environment and Child Development.* New York: Plenum Press, 1987.

Recommended Viewing

▼▼▼▼▼▼▼▼▼

The following videotapes, which illustrate concepts covered in this book, are recommended as additional teaching aids.

Color and Light: An Introduction. 1977. 11 minutes. Deerfield, Ill.: Coronet Films.
An introduction to the spectrum showing the relationship between black and white and color and light, primary colors and the effect of light on opaque, translucent and transparent materials.

Human Development: A New Look at the Infant. 1982. 30 minutes. Irvine, Calif.: Concept Media.

Part of a series, this segment provides an exploration of infant stimulus including people and inanimate objects.

Light. 1981. 15 minutes. Los Angeles: Direct Cinema Ltd., Inc.
A history of light from Genesis to Edison, showing the ways that sun, light and darkness have been represented through the ages and tracing the methods of artificial illumination.

Light Is Many Things. 1977. 12 minutes. Pasadena, Calif.: Barr Films.

Children experiment, observe, discover and enjoy light in many different ways.

Teach Me How I Can Do It Myself. 1971. 29 minutes. Chicago: International Film Bureau.
Learning according to the principles of Maria Montessori is demonstrated in a Dutch educational setting showing that the Montessori method is a total way of life which involves child, parents and teachers.

Index

Credits

Wallpaper designs used as part openers courtesy of Sunworthy Designs. Furnishings and ergonomics chart illustrations by Norm Nuding.

Room layout illustrations by Ray Barber, based on designs by Michael Cyckevic (10, 78, 92) and Steve Miller (18). Learning environment logos (136–43) by Rachel Geswaldo.

Preceding Text: ii J. Michael Kanouff; iv Fred Lyon. Reprinted from *Better Homes and Gardens* September, 1983. Copyright Meredith Corporation 1983. All rights reserved; xii S. Matoi.

Chapter 1: 11, 13, 14, Antonio F. Torrice; 12, Ray Scotty Morris.

Chapter 2: 19, 20, 21 (top right), 23 (bottom left), 24, 25, 29, Antonio F. Torrice; 21 (bottom left), 23 (top right) Fred Lyon. Reprinted from *Better Homes and Gardens* September, 1983. Copyright Meredith Corporation 1983. All rights reserved.

Chapter 3: 32, Paul Bielenberg; 34, 37 (bottom left), 38, 40 (top left) 44, 47, Mike Spinelli; 35, Dr. Mikol Davis; 37 top left) Greg de Lory; 37 (top right), 40 (bottom left) 41, 42, 43, 46, J. Michael Kanouff; 37 (bottom right) Stephen Marley; 50, Michael Staron.

Chapter 4: 54, 55, 56, 57, 66, 70 (bottom right), Fred Lyon, Reprinted from *Better Homes and Gardens* February, 1980. Copyright Meredith Corporation 1980. All rights reserved; 72, Fred Lyon, Reprinted from *Better Homes and Gardens* April, 1984. Copyright Meredith Corporation 1984. All rights reserved; 59 (top), Tom Virtue; 59 (bottom), 63, 64, 70 (bottom left), 73, 74, Mike Spinelli; 60, 61, 71, J. Michael Kanouff; 68, 69, Antonio F. Torrice.

Chapter 5: 80, Dennis Anderson; 81, 87 Antonio F. Torrice; 82, 84, Chuck Ashley, Reprinted from *Better Homes and Gardens Decorating* Summer, 1984. Copyright Meredith Corporation 1984. All rights reserved; 83, S. Matoi; 86, Mike Spinelli; 88, 89 Barrier Free Environments Inc., Raleigh, N.C.

Chapter 6: 94, Stephen Marley; 95, 96, 97, 99, 100, 101, J. Michael Kanouff.

Antonio F. Torrice, ASID is a leading authority on designing spaces for special needs. He is the recipient of several prestigious national honors, including the American Society of Interior Designers Human Environment Award and the Halo Contract Lighting Award, which recognized the pediatric solarium he designed for the Children's Hospital of San Francisco.

Torrice has founded two design firms. Just Between Friends tapped the interests of children by allowing them to co-design their spaces every step of the way. It was singled out by the Institute of International Education to commemorate the 1979 International Year of the Child. Living and Learning Environments reflects the scope of Torrice's work and encompasses the needs of the elderly and physically challenged. In 1987, Torrice represented the American Society of Interior Designers at the United Nations for World Children's Day.

In addition to lecturing nationwide, Torrice is an instructor at the Academy of Art College in San Francisco and on the international faculty at the Ontario College of Art in Toronto. He is a contributing editor of *Designers West*, and his column, co-written with Ro Logrippo, appears six times a year. His work has been featured in *Better Homes and Gardens*, *Good Housekeeping*, *USA Today*, *The Boston Globe*, *The Los Angeles Times*, and many other publications. A native of Massachusetts, Torrice is now based in San Francisco.

Ro Logrippo has been writing about the design world since the 1970s when she started covering home furnishings for *The San Mateo Times*, a daily newspaper in the San Francisco Bay Area. She is an Allied member of the American Society of Interior Designers.

During her career, the Marquette University College of Journalism graduate has earned numerous writing and layout awards, many related to design coverage, including first place in the Dallas Market Center's 1979 National Editorial Awards Competition.

Other recognitions include an international first-place award in 1983 from the International Reading Association for a story on teaching preschoolers to read, and first-place state honors in 1983, 1984, 1985, 1987, and 1988 awarded by the California Press Women.

She writes the bi-monthly *Designers West* column, "Designing for Special People," with Antonio F. Torrice, and shares directorship of Living and Learning Environments with him. Married to a commercial photographer, she is a Pennsylvania native who now resides in Burlingame, California. *In My Room* is her first book.

THE RAINBOW COLORED CARDS